PERT Practice!

Postsecondary Education Readiness Test Practice Questions

Published by

Blue Butterfly Books™

Published by

Blue Butterfly Books™
Victoria BC Canada

Printed in the USA

Team Members for this publication

Editor: Sheila M. Hynes, MES York, BA (Hons)
Contributor: Dr. C. Gregory
Contributor: Elizabeta Petrovic MSc (Mathematics)
Contributor: Kelley O'Malley BA (English)

ISBN-13: 978-0993753787 (Blue Butterfly Books)

ISBN-10: 0993753787

Version 6.5 May 2015

Sustainability and Eco-Responsibility

Here at *Blue Butterfly Books*^{TM}, trees are valuable to Mother Earth and the health and wellbeing of everyone. Minimizing our ecological footprint and effect on the environment, we choose Create Space, an eco-responsible printing company.

Electronic routing of our books reduces greenhouse gas emissions, worldwide. When a book order is received, the order is filled at the printing location closest to the client. Using environmentally friendly publishing technology of the Espresso book printing machine, *Blue Butterfly Books*^{TM} are printed as they are requested, saving thousands of books, and trees over time. This process offers the stable and viable alternative keeping healthy sustainability of our environment.

All paper is acid-free, and interior paper stock is made from 30% post-consumer waste recycled material. Safe for children, Create Space also verifies the materials used in the print process are all CPSIA-compliant.

By purchasing this *Blue Butterfly Books*^{TM}, you have supported Full Recovery and Preservation of The Karner Blue Butterfly . Our logo is the Karner Blue Butterfly, Lycaeides melissa samuelis, a rare and beautiful butterfly species whose only flower for propagation is the blue lupin flower. The Karner Butterfly is mostly found in the Great Lakes Region of the U.S.A. Recovery planning is in action, for the return of Karner Blue in Canada led by the National Recovery Strategy. The recovery goals and objectives are aimed at recreating suitable habitats for the butterfly and encourage the growth of blue lupines - the butterfly's natural ideal habitat.

For more info on the Karner Blue Butterfly , feel free to visit:

http://www.albanypinebush.org/conservation/wildlife-management/karner-blue-butterfly-recovery

http://www.wiltonpreserve.org/conservation/karner-blue-butterfly.

http://www.natureconservancy.ca/en/what-we-do/resource-centre/featured-species/karner_blue.html.

Contents

Getting Started

CONGRATULATIONS! By deciding to take the Florida Post Secondary Readiness Test (PERT), you have taken the first step toward a great future! Of course, there is no point in taking this important examination unless you intend to do your very best to earn the highest grade you possibly can. That means getting yourself organized and discovering the best approaches, methods and strategies to master the material. Yes, that will require real effort and dedication on your part but if you are willing to focus your energy and devote the study time necessary, before you know it you will be on you will be opening that letter of acceptance to the school of your dreams!

We know that taking on a new endeavour can be a little scary, and it is easy to feel unsure of where to begin. That's where we come in. This study guide is designed to help you improve your test-taking skills, show you a few tricks of the trade and increase both your competency and confidence.

The PERT Exam

The PERT exam is composed of three main sections, reading, mathematics, and writing. The reading section consists of reading comprehension, analysis of written passages and meaning in context. The mathematics section contains, arithmetic, algebra, geometry and polynomials and quadratic equations. The writing skills section contains questions on sentence structure and rewriting sentences. The writing section contains an essay question, as well as English grammar, spelling, punctuation and usage.

The PERT exam is computer based and adaptive. This means if you answer a questions correctly, the next question will be more difficulty until you reach your level of difficulty. If you answer incorrectly and you are not already at the lowest level of difficulty, the next question will be easier. Each question is multiple-choice, and the exact number of questions varies from student to student depending on how skilled the student is in a particular area.

While we seek to make our guide as comprehensive as possible, note that like all exams, the PERT Exam might be adjusted at some future point. New material might be added, or content that is no longer relevant or applicable might be removed. It is always a good idea to give the materials you receive when you register a careful review.

How this study guide is organized

This study guide is divided into three sections. The first section, self-assessments, which will help you recognize your areas of strength and weaknesses. This will be a boon when it comes to managing your study time most efficiently; there is not much point of focusing on material you have already got firmly under control. Instead, taking the self-assessments will show you where that time could be much better spent. In this area you will begin with a few questions to quickly evaluate your understanding of material that is likely to appear on the PERT. If you do poorly in certain areas, simply work carefully through those sections in the tutorials and then try the self-assessment again.

The second section, Tutorials, offers information in each of the content areas, as well as strategies to help you master that material. The tutorials are not intended to be a complete course, but cover general principles. If you find that you do not understand the tutorials, it is recommended that you seek out additional instruction.

Third, we offer two sets of practice test questions, similar to those on the PERT Exam.

The PERT Study Plan

Now that you have made the decision to take the PERT, it
is time to get started. Before you do another thing, you will
need to figure out a plan of attack. The very best study tip is
to start early! The longer the time period you devote to regular study practice, the more likely you will be to retain the
material and be able to access it quickly. If you thought that
1x20 is the same as 2x10, guess what? It really is not, when
it comes to study time. Reviewing material for just an hour
per day over the course of 20 days is far better than studying for two hours a day for only 10 days. The more often
you revisit a particular piece of information, the better you
will know it. Not only will your grasp and understanding be
better, but your ability to reach into your brain and quickly
and efficiently pull out the tidbit you need, will be greatly
enhanced as well.

The great Chinese scholar and philosopher Confucius be-
lieved that true knowledge could be defined as knowing
both what you know and what you do not know. The first
step in preparing for the PERT is to assess your strengths
and weaknesses. You may already have an idea of what you
know and what you do not know, but evaluating yourself
using our Self- Assessment modules for each of the three areas, Math, Writing and Reading Comprehension, will clarify
the details.

Making a Study Schedule

To make your study time most productive you will need to
develop a study plan. The purpose of the plan is to organize
all the bits of pieces of information in such a way that you
will not feel overwhelmed. Rome was not built in a day, and
learning everything you will need to know to pass the PERT
is going to take time, too. Arranging the material you need
to learn into manageable chunks is the best way to go. Each
study session should make you feel as though you have suc-

ceeded in accomplishing your goal, and your goal is simply to learn what you planned to learn during that particular session. Try to organize the content in such a way that each study session builds on previous ones. That way, you will retain the information, be better able to access it, and review the previous bits and pieces at the same time.

Self-assessment

The Best Study Tip! The very best study tip is to start early! The longer you study regularly, the more you will retain and 'learn' the material. Studying for 1 hour per day for 20 days is far better than studying for 2 hours for 10 days.

What don't you know?

The first step is to assess your strengths and weaknesses. You may already have an idea of where your weaknesses are, or you can take our Self-assessment modules for each of the areas, Reading Comprehension, Arithmetic, Essay Writing, Algebra and College Level Math.

Exam Component	Rate 1 to 5
Reading Comprehension	
Making Inferences	
Main idea	
Arithmetic	
Decimals Percent and Fractions	
Problem solving (Word Problems)	
Basic Algebra	
Simple Geometry	
Problem Solving	

Essay and English	
Essay Writing	
Basic English Grammar and Usage	
Spelling	
Punctuation	
Capitalization	
Mathematics	
Linear Equations	
Quadratics	
Polynomials	
Coordinate Geometry	

Making a Study Schedule

The key to making a study plan is to divide the material you need to learn into manageable size and learn it, while at the same time reviewing the material that you already know.

Using the table above, any scores of three or below, you need to spend time learning, going over, and practicing this subject area. A score of four means you need to review the material, but you don't have to spend time re-learning. A score of five and you are OK with just an occasional review before the exam.

A score of zero or one means you really do need to work on this and you should allocate the most time and give it the highest priority. Some students prefer a 5-day plan and others a 10-day plan. It also depends on how much time you have until the exam.

Here is an example of a 5-day plan based on an example from the table above:

Main Idea: 1   Study 1 hour everyday – review on last day
Linear Equations: 3   Study 1 hour for 2 days then ½ hour and then review
Algebra: 4   Review every second day

Grammar & Usage: 2 Study 1 hour on the first day – then ½ hour everyday
Reading Comprehension: 5   Review for ½ hour every other day
Geometry: 5 Review for ½ hour every other day

Using this example, geometry and reading comprehension are good and only need occasional review. Algebra is good and needs 'some' review. Linear Equations need a bit of work, grammar and usage needs a lot of work and Main Idea is very weak and need most of time. Based on this, here is a sample study plan:

Day	Subject	Time
Monday		
Study	Main Idea	1 hour
Study	Grammar & Usage	1 hour
	½ hour break	
Study	Linear Equations	1 hour
Review	Algebra	½ hour
Tuesday		
Study	Main Idea	1 hour
Study	Grammar & Usage	½ hour
	½ hour break	
Study	Linear Equations	½ hour
Review	Algebra	½ hour
Review	Geometry	½ hour
Wednesday		
Study	Main Idea	1 hour
Study	Grammar & Usage	½ hour
	½ hour break	
Study	Linear Equations	½ hour
Review	Geometry	½ hour
Thursday		
Study	Main Idea	½ hour
Study	Grammar & Usage	½ hour
Review	Linear Equations	½ hour
	½ hour break	
Review	Geometry	½ hour

Review	Algebra	½ hour
Friday		
Review	Main Idea	½ hour
Review	Grammar & Usage	½ hour
Review	Linear Equations	½ hour
	½ hour break	
Review	Algebra	½ hour
Review	Grammar & Usage	½ hour

Using this example, adapt the study plan to your own schedule. This schedule assumes 2 ½ - 3 hours available to study everyday for a 5 day period.

First, write out what you need to study and how much. Next figure out how many days you have before the test. Note, do NOT study on the last day before the test. On the last day before the test, you won't learn anything and will probably only confuse yourself.

Make a table with the days before the test and the number of hours you have available to study each day. We suggest working with 1 hour and ½ hour time slots.

Start filling in the blanks, with the subjects you need to study the most getting the most time and the most regular time slots (i.e. everyday) and the subjects that you know getting the least time (e.g. ½ hour every other day, or every 3rd day).

Tips for making a schedule

Once you make a schedule, stick with it! Make your study sessions reasonable. If you make a study schedule and don't stick with it, you set yourself up for failure. Instead, schedule study sessions that are a bit shorter and set yourself up for success! Make sure your study sessions are do-able. Studying is hard work but after you pass, you can party and take a break!

Schedule breaks. Breaks are just as important as study time. Work out a rotation of studying and breaks that works for you.

Build up study time. If you find it hard to sit still and study for 1 hour straight through, build up to it. Start with 20 minutes, and then take a break. Once you get used to 20-minute study sessions, increase the time to 30 minutes. Gradually work you way up to 1 hour.

40 minutes to 1 hour are optimal. Studying for longer than this is tiring and not productive. Studying for shorter isn't long enough to be productive.

Studying Math. Studying Math is different from studying other subjects because you use a different part of your brain. The best way to study math is to practice everyday. This will train your mind to think in a mathematical way. If you miss a day or days, the mathematical mind-set is gone and you have to start all over again to build it up.

Study and practice math everyday for at least 5 days before the exam.

Practice Test Questions Set 1

The questions below are not the same as you will find on the PERT - that would be too easy! And nobody knows what the questions will be and they change all the time. Below are general questions that cover the same subject areas as the PERT. So, while the format and exact wording of the questions may differ slightly, and change from year to year, if you can answer the questions below, you will have no problem with the PERT.

For the best results, take these practice test questions as if it were the real exam. Set aside time when you will not be disturbed, and a location that is quiet and free of distractions. Read the instructions carefully, read each question carefully, and answer to the best of your ability.
Use the bubble answer sheets provided. When you have completed the practice questions, check your answer against the Answer Key and read the explanation provided.

Do not attempt more than one set of practice test questions in one day. After completing the first practice test, wait two or three days before attempting the second set of questions.

Reading Answer Sheet

1. (A) (B) (C) (D)   11. (A) (B) (C) (D)   21. (A) (B) (C) (D)

2. (A) (B) (C) (D)   12. (A) (B) (C) (D)   22. (A) (B) (C) (D)

3. (A) (B) (C) (D)   13. (A) (B) (C) (D)   23. (A) (B) (C) (D)

4. (A) (B) (C) (D)   14. (A) (B) (C) (D)   24. (A) (B) (C) (D)

5. (A) (B) (C) (D)   15. (A) (B) (C) (D)   25. (A) (B) (C) (D)

6. (A) (B) (C) (D)   16. (A) (B) (C) (D)   26. (A) (B) (C) (D)

7. (A) (B) (C) (D)   17. (A) (B) (C) (D)   27. (A) (B) (C) (D)

8. (A) (B) (C) (D)   18. (A) (B) (C) (D)   28. (A) (B) (C) (D)

9. (A) (B) (C) (D)   19. (A) (B) (C) (D)   29. (A) (B) (C) (D)

10. (A) (B) (C) (D)   20. (A) (B) (C) (D)   30. (A) (B) (C) (D)

Mathematics Answer Sheet

1. Ⓐ Ⓑ Ⓒ Ⓓ   11. Ⓐ Ⓑ Ⓒ Ⓓ   21. Ⓐ Ⓑ Ⓒ Ⓓ

2. Ⓐ Ⓑ Ⓒ Ⓓ   12. Ⓐ Ⓑ Ⓒ Ⓓ   22. Ⓐ Ⓑ Ⓒ Ⓓ

3. Ⓐ Ⓑ Ⓒ Ⓓ   13. Ⓐ Ⓑ Ⓒ Ⓓ   23. Ⓐ Ⓑ Ⓒ Ⓓ

4. Ⓐ Ⓑ Ⓒ Ⓓ   14. Ⓐ Ⓑ Ⓒ Ⓓ   24. Ⓐ Ⓑ Ⓒ Ⓓ

5. Ⓐ Ⓑ Ⓒ Ⓓ   15. Ⓐ Ⓑ Ⓒ Ⓓ   25. Ⓐ Ⓑ Ⓒ Ⓓ

6. Ⓐ Ⓑ Ⓒ Ⓓ   16. Ⓐ Ⓑ Ⓒ Ⓓ   26. Ⓐ Ⓑ Ⓒ Ⓓ

7. Ⓐ Ⓑ Ⓒ Ⓓ   17. Ⓐ Ⓑ Ⓒ Ⓓ   27. Ⓐ Ⓑ Ⓒ Ⓓ

8. Ⓐ Ⓑ Ⓒ Ⓓ   18. Ⓐ Ⓑ Ⓒ Ⓓ   28. Ⓐ Ⓑ Ⓒ Ⓓ

9. Ⓐ Ⓑ Ⓒ Ⓓ   19. Ⓐ Ⓑ Ⓒ Ⓓ   29. Ⓐ Ⓑ Ⓒ Ⓓ

10. Ⓐ Ⓑ Ⓒ Ⓓ   20. Ⓐ Ⓑ Ⓒ Ⓓ   30. Ⓐ Ⓑ Ⓒ Ⓓ

Writing Skills Answer Sheet

1. (A) (B) (C) (D)   11. (A) (B) (C) (D)   21. (A) (B) (C) (D)

2. (A) (B) (C) (D)   12. (A) (B) (C) (D)   22. (A) (B) (C) (D)

3. (A) (B) (C) (D)   13. (A) (B) (C) (D)   23. (A) (B) (C) (D)

4. (A) (B) (C) (D)   14. (A) (B) (C) (D)   24. (A) (B) (C) (D)

5. (A) (B) (C) (D)   15. (A) (B) (C) (D)   25. (A) (B) (C) (D)

6. (A) (B) (C) (D)   16. (A) (B) (C) (D)   26. (A) (B) (C) (D)

7. (A) (B) (C) (D)   17. (A) (B) (C) (D)   27. (A) (B) (C) (D)

8. (A) (B) (C) (D)   18. (A) (B) (C) (D)   28. (A) (B) (C) (D)

9. (A) (B) (C) (D)   19. (A) (B) (C) (D)   29. (A) (B) (C) (D)

10. (A) (B) (C) (D)   20. (A) (B) (C) (D)   30. (A) (B) (C) (D)

Part 1 - Reading

Questions 1 – 4 refer to the following passage.

Infectious Diseases

An infectious disease is a clinically evident illness resulting from the presence of pathogenic agents, such as viruses, bacteria, fungi, protozoa, multi-cellular parasites, and unusual proteins known as prions. Infectious pathologies are also called communicable diseases or transmissible diseases, due to their potential of transmission from one person or species to another by a replicating agent (as opposed to a toxin).

Transmission of an infectious disease can occur in many different ways. Physical contact, liquids, food, body fluids, contaminated objects, and airborne inhalation can all transmit infecting agents.

Transmissible diseases that occur through contact with an ill person, or objects touched by them, are especially infective, and are sometimes called contagious diseases. Communicable diseases that require a more specialized route of infection, such as through blood or needle transmission, or sexual transmission, are usually not regarded as contagious.

The term infectivity describes the ability of an organism to enter, survive and multiply in the host, while the infectiousness of a disease indicates the comparative ease with which the disease is transmitted. An infection however, is not synonymous with an infectious disease, as an infection may not cause important clinical symptoms. [3]

1. What can we infer from the first paragraph in this passage?

a. Sickness from a toxin can be easily transmitted from one person to another.

b. Sickness from an infectious disease can be easily transmitted from one person to another.

c. Few sicknesses are transmitted from one person to another.

d. Infectious diseases are easily treated.

2. What are two other names for infections' pathologies?

a. Communicable diseases or transmissible diseases

b. Communicable diseases or terminal diseases

c. Transmissible diseases or preventable diseases

d. Communicative diseases or unstable diseases

3. What does infectivity describe?

a. The inability of an organism to multiply in the host.

b. The inability of an organism to reproduce.

c. The ability of an organism to enter, survive and multiply in the host.

d. The ability of an organism to reproduce in the host.

4. How do we know an infection is not synonymous with an infectious disease?

a. Because an infectious disease destroys infections with enough time.

b. Because an infection may not cause clinical symptoms or impair host function.

c. We do not. The two are synonymous.

d. Because an infection is too fatal to be an infectious disease.

Questions 5 – 7 refer to the following passage.

Thunderstorms

The first stage of a thunderstorm is the cumulus stage, or developing stage. In this stage, masses of moisture are lifted upwards into the atmosphere. The trigger for this lift can be insulation heating the ground producing thermals, areas where two winds converge, forcing air upwards, or, where winds blow over terrain of increasing elevation. Moisture in the air rapidly cools into liquid drops of water, which appears as cumulus clouds.

As the water vapor condenses into liquid, latent heat is released which warms the air, causing it to become less dense than the surrounding dry air. The warm air rises in an updraft through the process of convection (hence the term convective precipitation). This creates a low-pressure zone beneath the forming thunderstorm. In a typical thunderstorm, about 5×10^8 kg of water vapor is lifted, and the quantity of energy released when this condenses is about equal to the energy used by a city of 100,000 in a month. [4]

5. The cumulus stage of a thunderstorm is the

    a. The last stage of the storm.

    b. The middle stage of the storm formation.

    c. The beginning of the thunderstorm.

    d. The period after the thunderstorm has ended.

6. One way the air is warmed is

    a. Air moving downwards, which creates a high-pressure zone.

    b. Air cooling and becoming less dense, causing it to rise.

    c. Moisture moving downward toward the earth.

    d. Heat created by water vapor condensing into liquid.

7. Identify the correct sequence of events.

a. Warm air rises, water droplets condense, creating more heat, and the air rises farther.

b. Warm air rises and cools, water droplets condense, causing low pressure.

c. Warm air rises and collects water vapor, the water vapor condenses as the air rises, which creates heat, and causes the air to rise farther.

d. None of the above.

Questions 8 – 10 refer to the following passage.

The US Weather Service

The United States National Weather Service classifies thunderstorms as severe when they reach a predetermined level. Usually, this means the storm is strong enough to inflict wind or hail damage. In most of the United States, a storm is considered severe if winds reach over 50 knots (58 mph or 93 km/h), hail is ¾ inch (2 cm) diameter or larger, or if meteorologists report funnel clouds or tornadoes. In the Central Region of the United States National Weather Service, the hail threshold for a severe thunderstorm is 1 inch (2.5 cm) in diameter. Though a funnel cloud or tornado indicates the presence of a severe thunderstorm, the various meteorological agencies would issue a tornado warning rather than a severe thunderstorm warning here.

Meteorologists in Canada define a severe thunderstorm as either having tornadoes, wind gusts of 90 km/h or greater, hail 2 centimeters in diameter or greater, rainfall more than 50 millimeters in 1 hour, or 75 millimeters in 3 hours.

Severe thunderstorms can develop from any type of thunderstorm. [5]

8. What is the purpose of this passage?

    a. Explaining when a thunderstorm turns into a tornado.

    b. Explaining who issues storm warnings, and when these warnings should be issued.

    c. Explaining when meteorologists consider a thunderstorm severe.

    d. None of the above.

9. It is possible to infer from this passage that

    a. Different areas and countries have different criteria for determining a severe storm.

    b. Thunderstorms can include lightning and tornadoes, as well as violent winds and large hail.

    c. If someone spots both a thunderstorm and a tornado, meteorological agencies will immediately issue a severe storm warning.

    d. Canada has a much different alert system for severe storms, with criteria that are far less.

10. What would the Central Region of the United States National Weather Service do if hail was 2.7 cm in diameter?

    a. Not issue a severe thunderstorm warning.

    b. Issue a tornado warning.

    c. Issue a severe thunderstorm warning.

    d. Sleet must also accompany the hail before the Weather Service will issue a storm warning.

Questions 11 – 13 refer to the following passage.

Clouds

A cloud is a visible mass of droplets or frozen crystals floating in the atmosphere above the surface of the Earth or other planetary bodies. Another type of cloud is a mass of material in space, attracted by gravity, called interstellar clouds and nebulae. The branch of meteorology which studies clouds is called nephrology. When we are speaking of Earth clouds, water vapor is usually the condensing substance, which forms small droplets or ice crystal. These crystals are typically 0.01 mm in diameter. Dense, deep clouds reflect most light, so they appear white, at least from the top. Cloud droplets scatter light very efficiently, so the farther into a cloud light travels, the weaker it gets. This accounts for the gray or dark appearance at the base of large clouds. Thin clouds may appear to have acquired the color of their environment or background. [6]

11. What are clouds made of?

    a. Water droplets

    b. Ice crystals

    c. Ice crystals and water droplets

    d. Clouds on Earth are made of ice crystals and water droplets

12. The main idea of this passage is

    a. Condensation occurs in clouds, having an intense effect on the weather on the surface of the earth.

    b. Atmospheric gases are responsible for the gray color of clouds just before a severe storm happens.

    c. A cloud is a visible mass of droplets or frozen crystals floating in the atmosphere above the surface of the Earth or other planetary body.

    d. Clouds reflect light in varying amounts and degrees, depending on the size and concentration of the water droplets.

13. Why are clouds white on top and grey on the bottom?

a. Because water droplets inside the cloud do not reflect light, it appears white, and the farther into the cloud the light travels, the less light is reflected making the bottom appear dark.

b. Because water droplets outside the cloud reflect light, it appears dark, and the farther into the cloud the light travels, the more light is reflected making the bottom appear white.

c. Because water droplets inside the cloud reflects light, making it appear white, and the farther into the cloud the light travels, the more light is reflected making the bottom appear dark.

d. None of the above.

Questions 14 - 17 refer to the following passage.

Keeping Tropical Fish

Keeping tropical fish at home or in your office used to be very popular. Today, interest has declined, but it remains as rewarding and relaxing a hobby as ever. Ask any tropical fish hobbyist, and you will hear how soothing and relaxing watching colorful fish live their lives in the aquarium. If you are considering keeping tropical fish as pets, here is a list of the basic equipment you will need.

A filter is essential for keeping your aquarium clean and your fish alive and healthy. There are different types and sizes of filters and the right size for you depends on the size of the aquarium and the level of stocking. Generally, you need a filter with a 3 to 5 times turn over rate per hour. This means that the water in the tank should go through the filter about 3 to 5 times per hour.

Most tropical fish do well in water temperatures ranging between 24°C and 26°C, though each has its own ideal water temperature. A heater with a thermostat is necessary to regulate the water temperature. Some heaters are submersible and others are not, so check carefully before you buy.

Lights are also necessary, and come in a large variety of types, strengths and sizes. A light source is necessary for plants in the tank to photosynthesize and give the tank a more attractive appearance. Even if you plan to use plastic plants, the fish still require light, although here you can use a lower strength light source.

A hood is necessary to keep dust, dirt and unwanted materials out of the tank. Sometimes the hood can also help prevent evaporation. Another requirement is aquarium gravel. This will improve the aesthetics of the aquarium and is necessary if you plan to have real plants.

14. What is the general tone of this article?

    a. Formal

    b. Informal

    c. Technical

    d. Opinion

15. Which of the following can not be inferred?

    a. Gravel is good for aquarium plants.

    b. Fewer people have aquariums in their office than at home.

    c. The larger the tank, the larger the filter required.

    d. None of the above.

16. What evidence does the author provide to support their claim that aquarium lights are necessary?

    a. Plants require light.

    b. Fish and plants require light.

    c. The author does not provide evidence for this statement.

    d. Aquarium lights make the aquarium more attractive.

17. Which of the following is an opinion?

a. Filter with a 3 to 5 times turn over rate per hour are required.

b. Aquarium gravel improves the aesthetics of the aquarium.

c. An aquarium hood keeps dust, dirt and unwanted materials out of the tank.

d. Each type of tropical fish has its own ideal water temperature.

Questions 18 - 20 refer to the following passage.

Ways Characters Communicate in Theater

Playwrights give their characters voices in a way that gives depth and added meaning to what happens on stage during their play. There are different types of speech in scripts that allow characters to talk with themselves, with other characters, and even with the audience.

It is very unique to theater that characters may talk "to themselves." When characters do this, the speech they give is called a soliloquy. Soliloquies are usually poetic, introspective, moving, and can tell audience members about the feelings, motivations, or suspicions of an individual character without that character having to reveal them to other characters on stage. "To be or not to be" is a famous soliloquy given by Hamlet as he considers difficult but important themes, such as life and death.

The most common type of communication in plays is when one character is speaking to another or a group of other characters. This is generally called dialogue, but can also be called monologue if one character speaks without being interrupted for a long time. It is not necessarily the most important type of communication, but it is the most common because the plot of the play cannot really progress without it.

Lastly, and most unique to theater (although it has been

used somewhat in film) is when a character speaks directly to the audience. This is called an aside, and scripts usually specifically direct actors to do this. Asides are usually comical, an inside joke between the character and the audience, and very short. The actor will usually face the audience when delivering them, even if it's for a moment, so the audience can recognize this move as an aside.

All three of these types of communication are important to the art of theater, and have been perfected by famous playwrights like Shakespeare. Understanding these types of communication can help an audience member grasp what is artful about the script and action of a play. [7]

18. According to the passage, characters in plays communicate to

    a. move the plot forward

    b. show the private thoughts and feelings of one character

    c. make the audience laugh

    d. add beauty and artistry to the play

19. When Hamlet delivers "To be or not to be," he can most likely be described as

    a. solitary

    b. thoughtful

    c. dramatic

    d. hopeless

20. The author uses parentheses to punctuate "although it has been used somewhat in film"

a. to show that films are less important

b. instead of using commas so that the sentence is not interrupted

c. because parenthesis help separate details that are not as important

d. to show that films are not as artistic

Questions 21 - 24 refer to the following passage.

Frankenstein

Great God! What a scene has just taken place! I am yet dizzy with the remembrance of it. I hardly know whether I shall have the power to detail it; yet the tale which I have recorded would be incomplete without this final and wonderful catastrophe. I entered the cabin where lay the remains of my ill-fated and admirable friend. Over him hung a form which I cannot find words to describe—gigantic in stature, yet uncouth and distorted in its proportions. As he hung over the coffin, his face was concealed by long locks of ragged hair; but one vast hand was extended, in color and apparent texture like that of a mummy. When he heard the sound of my approach, he ceased to utter exclamations of grief and horror and sprung towards the window. Never did I behold a vision so horrible as his face, of such loathsome yet appalling hideousness. I shut my eyes involuntarily and endeavored to recollect what were my duties with regard to this destroyer. I called on him to stay.

He paused, looking on me with wonder, and again turning towards the lifeless form of his creator, he seemed to forget my presence, and every feature and gesture seemed instigated by the wildest rage of some uncontrollable passion.

"That is also my victim!" he exclaimed. "In his murder my crimes are consummated; the miserable series of my being is wound to its close! Oh, Frankenstein! Generous and self-devoted being! What does it avail that I now ask thee to pardon me? I, who irretrievably destroyed thee by destroying all thou lovedst. Alas! He is cold, he cannot answer me."

His voice seemed suffocated, and my first impulses, which had suggested to me the duty of obeying the dying request of my friend in destroying his enemy, were now suspended by a mixture of curiosity and compassion. I approached this tremendous being; I dared not again raise my eyes to his face, there was something so scaring and unearthly in his ugliness. I attempted to speak, but the words died away on my lips. The monster continued to utter wild and incoherent self-reproaches. At length I gathered resolution to address him in a pause of the tempest of his passion.

"Your repentance," I said, "is now superfluous. If you had listened to the voice of conscience and heeded the stings of remorse before you had urged your diabolical vengeance to this extremity, Frankenstein would yet have lived." [7]

21. Who is the "ill-fated and admirable friend" who is lying in the coffin?

    a. Frankenstein's monster

    b. Frankenstein

    c. Mary Shelley

    d. Unknown

22. Why is the speaker 'suspended" from following through on his duty to destroy the monster?

    a. The way the monster looks

    b. The monster's remorse

    c. Curiosity and compassion

    d. Fear the monster might kill him too

23. How does Frankenstein's monster destroy Frankenstein?

    a. By killing Frankenstein

    b. By letting himself be the monster everyone sees him as

    c. By destroying everything Frankenstein loved

    d. All of the above

24. When the Speaker says the monster's repentance is "superfluous, what does he mean?

    a. That it is unnecessary and unused because Frankenstein is already dead and cannot hear him

    b. That he accepts the repentance on behalf of Frankenstein

    c. That the monster does not actually feel remorseful

    d. That his repentance is unneeded because he did not do anything wrong

Questions 25 - 26 refer to the following passage.

Scotland's Windy Power Source

The Scottish Government has a targeted plan of generating 100% of Scotland's electricity through renewable energy by 2020. Renewable energy sources include sun, water and wind power. Scotland uses all forms but its fastest growing energy is wind energy. Wind power is generated through the use of wind turbines, placed onshore and offshore. Wind turbines that are grouped together in large numbers are called wind farms. Most Scottish citizens say that the wind farms are necessary to meet current and future energy needs, and would like to see an increase in the number of wind farms. They cite the fact that wind energy does not cause pollution, there are low operational costs, and most importantly due to the definition of renewable energy it cannot be depleted.

25. What is Scotland's fastest growing source of renewable energy?

a. Solar Panels

b. Hydroelectric

c. Wind

d. Fossil Fuels

26. Why do most Scottish citizens agree with the Government's plan?

a. Their concern for current and future energy needs

b. Because of the low operational costs

c. Because they are out of sight

d. Because it provides jobs

Questions 27 - 28 refer to the following passage.

Scotland's Windy Power Source II

However, there is still a public debate concerning the use of wind farms to generate energy. The most cited argument against wind energy is that the up front investment is expensive. They also argue that it is aesthetically displeasing, they are noisy, and they create a serious threat to wildlife in the area. While wind energy is renewable, or cannot be depleted, it does not mean that wind is always available. Wind is fluctuating, or intermittent, and therefore not suited to meet the base amount of energy demand, meaning if there is no wind then no energy is being created.

27. What is the biggest argument against wind energy?

a. The turbines are noisy

b. The turbines endanger wildlife

c. The turbines are expensive to build

d. They are aesthetically displeasing

28. What is the best way to describe this article's description of wind energy?

    a. Loud and ever present

    b. The cheapest form of renewable energy

    c. The only source of renewable energy in Scotland

    d. Clean and renewable but fluctuating

Questions 29 - 30 refer to the following passage.

The Civil War

The Civil War began on April 12, 1861. The first shots of the Civil War were fired in Fort Sumter, South Carolina. Note that even though more American lives were lost in the Civil War than in any other war, not one person died on that first day. The war began because eleven Southern states seceded from the Union and tried to start their own government, The Confederate States of America.

Why did the states secede? The issue of slavery was a primary cause of the Civil War. The eleven southern states relied heavily on their slaves to foster their farming and plantation lifestyles. The northern states, many of whom had already abolished slavery, did not feel that the southern states should have slaves. The north wanted to free all the slaves and President Lincoln's goal was to both end slavery and preserve the Union. He had Congress declare war on the Confederacy on April 14, 1862. For four long, blood soaked years, the North and South fought.

From 1861 to mid 1863, it seemed as if the South would win this war. However, on July 1, 1863, an epic three day battle was waged on a field in Gettysburg, Pennsylvania. Gettysburg is remembered for being the bloodiest battle in American history. At the end of the three days, the North turned the tide of the war in their favor. The North then went onto dominate the South for the remainder of the war. Most well remembered might be General Sherman's "March to The Sea," where he famously led the Union Army through Georgia and the Carolinas, burning and destroying everything in their path.

In 1865, the Union army invaded and captured the Confederate capital of Richmond Virginia. Robert E. Lee, leader of the Confederacy surrendered to General Ulysses S. Grant, leader of the Union forces, on April 9, 1865. The Civil War was over, and the Union was preserved.

29. What does the word secede most nearly mean?

    a. To break away from

    b. To accomplish

    c. To join

    d. To lose

30. Which of the following statements summarizes a FACT from the passage?

    a. Congress declared war and then the Battle of Fort Sumter began.

    b. Congress declared war after shots were fired at Fort Sumter.

    c. President Lincoln was pro slavery

    d. President Lincoln was at Fort Sumter with Congress

AK = 58

PERT Review!

Mathematics

1. Divide 243 by 3^3

    a. 243

    b. 11

    c. 9

    d. 27

2. Solve the following equation $4(y + 6) = 3y + 30$

    a. $y = 20$

    b. $y = 6$

    c. $y = 30/7$

    d. $y = 30$

3. Divide $x^2 - y^2$ by $x - y$.

    a. $x - y$

    b. $x + y$

    c. xy

    d. $y - x$

4. Solve for x if, $10^2 \times 100^2 = 1000^x$

    a. $x = 2$

    b. $x = 3$

    c. $x = -2$

    d. $x = 0$

5. Given polynomials A = -2x⁴ + x² - 3x, B = x⁴ - x³ + 5 and C = x⁴ + 2x³ + 4x + 5, find A + B - C.

    a. $x^3 + x^2 + x + 10$

    b. $-3x^3 + x^2 - 7x + 10$

    c. $-2x^4 - 3x^3 + x^2 - 7x$

    d. $-3x^4 + x^3 + 2 - 7x$

6. Solve the inequality: $(x - 6)^2 \geq x^2 + 12$

    a. $(2, +\infty)$

    b. $(2, +\infty)$

    c. $(-\infty, 2]$

    d. $(12, +\infty)$

7. $7^5 - 3^5 =$

    a. 15,000

    b. 16,564

    c. 15,800

    d. 15,007

8. Divide $x^3 - 3x^2 + 3x - 1$ by x - 1.

    a. $x^2 - 1$

    b. $x^2 + 1$

    c. $x^2 - 2x + 1$

    d. $x^2 + 2x + 1$

9. Express 9 x 9 x 9 in exponential form and standard form.

    a. $9^3 = 719$

    b. $9^3 = 629$

    c. $9^3 = 729$

    d. $10^3 = 729$

10. Using the factoring method, solve the quadratic equation: $x^2 - 5x - 6 = 0$

    a. -6 and 1
    b. -1 and 6
    c. 1 and 6
    d. -6 and -1

11. Divide 0.524 by 10^3

    a. 0.0524
    b. 0.000524
    c. 0.00524
    d. 524

12. Factor the polynomial $x^3y^3 - x^2y^8$.

    a. $x^2y^3(x - y^5)$
    b. $x^3y^3(1 - y^5)$
    c. $x^2y^2(x - y^6)$
    d. $xy^3(x - y^5)$

13. Find the solution for the following linear equation: $5x/2 = 3x + 24/6$

    a. -1
    b. 0
    c. 1
    d. 2

14. 3^2 x 3^5

    a. 3^{17}
    b. 3^5
    c. 4^8
    d. 3^7

15. Solve the system, if a is some real number:

ax + y = 1
x + ay = 1

    a. (1,a)

    b. (1/a + 1, 1)

    c. (1/(a + 1), 1/(a + 1))

    d. (a, 1/a + 1)

16. Solve $3^5 \div 3^8$

    a. 3^3

    b. 3^5

    c. 3^6

    d. 3^4

17. Solve the linear equation: 3(x + 2) - 2(1 - x) = 4x + 5

    a. -1

    b. 0

    c. 1

    d. 2

18. Simplify the following expression: $3x^a + 6a^x - x^a + (-5a^x) - 2x^a$

    a. $a^x + x^a$

    b. $a^x - x^a$

    c. a^x

    d. x^a

19. Add polynomials $-3x^2 + 2x + 6$ and $-x^2 - x - 1$.

    a. $-2x^2 + x + 5$

    b. $-4x^2 + x + 5$

    c. $-2x^2 + 3x + 5$

    d. $-4x^2 + 3x + 5$

20. 10^4 is not equal to which of the following?

    a. 100,000

    b. 10 x 10 x 10 x 10

    c. $10^2 \times 10^2$

    d. 10,000

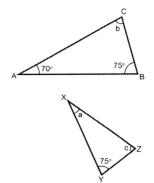

21. What are the respective values of a, b & c if both triangles are similar?

    a. 70°, 70°, 35°

    b. 70°, 35°, 70°

    c. 35°, 35°, 35°

    d. 70°, 35°, 35°

22. Consider 2 triangles, ABC and A'B'C', where:

BC = B' C'

AC = A' C'

RA = RA'

Are these 2 triangles congruent?

(a) Yes

b. No

c. Not enough information

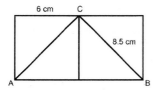

Note: figure not drawn to scale

23. Assuming the 2 quadrangles in the figure above are identical rectangles, what is the perimeter of △ABC in the above shape?

a. 25.5 cm

b. 27 cm

c. 30 cm

d. 29 cm

24. If angle α is equal to the expression 3π/2 - π/6 - π - π/3, find sinα.

(a) 0

b. 1/2

c. 1

d. 3/2

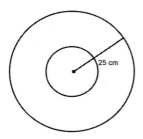

Note: figure not drawn to scale

25. What is the distance travelled by the wheel above, when it makes 175 revolutions?

    a. 87.5 π m
    b. 875 π m
    c. 8.75 π m
    d. 8750 π m

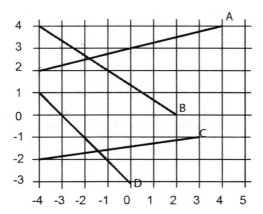

26. Which of the lines above represents the equation 2y – x = 4?

   (a) A

   b. B

   c. C

   d. D

27. Find the sides of a right triangle whose sides are consecutive numbers.

   a. 1, 2, 3

   b. 2, 3, 4

   (c) 3, 4, 5

   d. 4, 5, 6

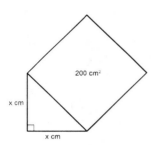

Note: figure not drawn to scale

28. Assuming the quadrangle in the figure above is a square, what is the length of the sides in the triangle above?

   (a) 10

   b. 20

   c. 100

   d. 40

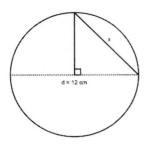

Note: figure not drawn to scale

29. Calculate the length of side x.

    a. 6.46
    b. 8.46
    c. 3.6
    d. 6.4

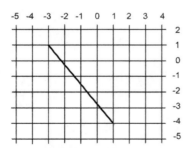

30. What is the slope of the line shown above?

    a. 5/4
    b. -4/5
    c. -5/4
    d. -4/5

Writing

Directions: For questions 1 - 3, read the short passage answer the question.

Alvin Lee began playing guitar at an early age, and was influenced by his parents' passion for music and inspired by the likes of Chuck Berry and Scotty Moore. [1] Lee started his career as the lead vocalist and guitarist in a band named the Jaybirds at the famous Marquee Club in London in 1962. [2] A few years later the band changed its name to Ten Years After, and released its debut album under the new name. [3] Lee's lightning fast guitar playing at the Woodstock Festival gained him instant stardom and Lee was asked to tour the US. [4]

1. Which sentence in the second paragraph is the least relevant to the main idea of the second paragraph?

    a. 1
    b. 2
    c. 3
    d. 4

Curiosity was launched in late November 2011 from Cape Canaveral Air Force Station in Florida. [1] It successfully landed on Mars on August 6, 2012 searching for evidence of life. [2] The car sized robot, weighing about a ton, is equipped with all the technical capacities to carry out its mission to explore our neighbor for biological, geological and geochemical traces of life. [3] It will also test the Martian soil and surface to collect data about its planetary evolution and surface radiation. [4]

2. Which sentence is the least relevant to the main idea of the third paragraph?

    a. 1

    b. 2

    c. 3

    d. 4

With an estimated 100,000 species, trees represent 25 percent of all living plant species. Most tree species grow in tropical regions of the world and many of these areas have not been surveyed by botanists, making species diversity poorly understood. The earliest trees were tree ferns and horsetails, which grew in forests in the Carboniferous period. Tree ferns still survive, but the only surviving horsetails are no longer in tree form. Later, in the Triassic period, conifers and ginkgos, appeared, followed by flowering plants after that in the Cretaceous period. [5]

3. Choose the correct list below, ranked from oldest to youngest trees.

    a. Flowering plants, conifers and ginkgos, tree ferns and horsetails

    b. Tree ferns and horsetails, conifers and ginkgos, flowering plants

    c. Tree ferns and horsetails, flowering plants, conifers and ginkgos

    d. Conifers and ginkgos, tree ferns and horsetails, flowering plants

Directions: Choose the word or phrase that best completes the sentence.

4. The Ford Motor Company was named for Henry Ford, _____ had founded the company.

     a. which

     b. who

     c. whose

     d. None of the options are correct.

5. Thomas Edison _____ as the greatest inventor since he invented the light bulb, television, motion pictures, and phonograph.

     a. has always been known

     b. was always been known

     c. must have had been always known

     d. None of the options are correct.

6. The weatherman on Channel 6 said that this has been the _____ summer on record.

     a. most hottest

     b. hottest

     c. hotter

     d. None of the options are correct.

7. Although Joe is tall for his age, his brother Elliot is _____ of the two.

     a. tallest

     b. tall of the two.

     c. the taller

     d. None of the options are correct.

8. When KISS came to town, all the tickets _____ sold out before I could buy one.

> a. will be
>
> b. had been
>
> c. were being
>
> d. None of the options are correct.

9. The rules of most sports _____ more complicated than we often realize.

> a. are
>
> b. is
>
> c. was
>
> d. None of the options are correct.

10. Neither of the Wright Brothers _____ any doubts that they would be successful with their flying machine.

> a. have
>
> b. has
>
> c. had
>
> d. None of the options are correct.

11. The Titanic _____ mere days into its maiden voyage.

> a. will already sunk
>
> b. sank
>
> c. had sank
>
> d. None of the choices are correct.

12. When he's _____ friends, Robert seems confident.

    a. None of the choices are correct.

    b. between

    c. among

13. His home was _____ than we expected.

    a. The sentence is correct.

    b. farther

    c. None of the choices are correct.

14. The tables were _____ by the students.

    a. laid

    b. lay

    c. lie

    d. None of the choices are correct.

15. Each boy and girl _____ given a toy.

    a. were

    b. was

    c. Either A or B can be used.

    d. None of the choices are correct.

16. His measles _____ getting better.

    a. is

    b. are

    c. Either A or B can be used.

    d. None of the choices are correct.

17. Despite the bad weather yesterday, he ____ still attend the party.

    a. The sentence is correct.

    b. could

    c. may

    d. None of the choices are correct.

18. Choose the sentence with the correct punctuation.

    a. To make chicken soup you must first buy a chicken.

    b. To make chicken soup you must first, buy a chicken.

    c. To make chicken soup, you must first buy a chicken.

    d. None of the choices are correct.

19. Choose the sentence with the correct punctuation.

    a. To travel around the globe, you have to drive 25000 miles.

    b. To travel around the globe, you have to drive, 25000 miles.

    c. None of the choices are correct.

    d. To travel around the globe, you have to drive 25,000 miles.

20. Choose the sentence with the correct punctuation.

    a. The dog loved chasing bones, but never ate them; it was running that he enjoyed.

    b. The dog loved chasing bones; but never ate them, it was running that he enjoyed.

    c. The dog loved chasing bones, but never ate them, it was running that he enjoyed.

    d. None of the choices are correct.

21. Choose the sentence with the correct punctuation.

    a. However, I believe that he didn't really try that hard.

    b. However I believe that he didn't really try that hard.

    c. None of the choices are correct.

    d. However: I believe that he didn't really try that hard.

22. Choose the sentence that is written correctly.

    a. Any girl that fails the test loses their admission.

    b. Any girl that fails the test loses our admission.

    c. Any girl that fails the test loses <u>her</u> admission.

    d. None of the choices are correct.

23. Choose the sentence that is written correctly.

    a. He ought to be back by now.

    b. He ought be back by now.

    c. He ought come back by now.

    d. None of the choices are correct.

24. Choose the sentence that is written correctly.

    a. The man as well as his son has arrived

    b. The man as well as his son have arrived.

    c. None of the choices are correct.

25. Choose the sentence that is written correctly.

    a. Mark and Peter have talked to each other.

    b. Mark and Peter have talked to one another.

    c. None of the choices are correct.

26. Choose the sentence that is written correctly.

    a. Christians believe that their lord have raised.

    b. Christians believe that their lord has risen.

    c. Christians believe that their lord have raise.

    d. None of the choices are correct.

27. Choose the sentence that is written correctly.

    a. Here are the names of people whom you should contact.

    b. Here are the names of people who you should contact

    c. None of the choices are correct.

28. Choose the sentence that is written correctly.

    a. The World Health Organization (WHO) are meeting by January.

    b. The World Health Organization (WHO) is meeting by January.

    c. None of the choices are correct.

29. Choose the sentence that is written correctly.

    a. They will have to retire when they reach 60 years of age.

    b. They shall have to retire when they reach 60 years of age.

    c. None of the choices are correct.

Directions: Choose the sentence that best support the topic sentence below.

30. Volcanoes occur because the planet's crust is broken into 17 major tectonic plates that float on a hotter, softer layer in the Earth's mantle.

a. Therefore, volcanoes are generally found where tectonic plates are diverging or converging.

b. Volcanoes generally cause extensive damage to property.

c. Volcanoes do not often erupt, but can be spectacular when they do.

c. Most volcanoes are far from major urban centers.

Answer Key

Reading

1. B
We can infer from this passage that sickness from an infectious disease can be easily transmitted from one person to another.

From the passage, "Infectious pathologies are also called communicable diseases or transmissible diseases, due to their potential of transmission from one person or species to another by a replicating agent (as opposed to a toxin)."

2. A
Two other names for infectious pathologies are communicable diseases and transmissible diseases.

From the passage, "Infectious pathologies are also called communicable diseases or transmissible diseases, due to their potential of transmission from one person or species to another by a replicating agent (as opposed to a toxin)."

3. C
Infectivity describes the ability of an organism to enter, survive and multiply in the host. This is taken directly from the passage, and is a definition type question.

Definition type questions can be answered quickly and easily by scanning the passage for the word you are asked to define.

"Infectivity" is an unusual word, so it is quick and easy to scan the passage looking for this word.

4. B
We know an infection is not synonymous with an infectious disease because an infection may not cause important clinical symptoms or impair host function.

5. C
The cumulus stage of a thunderstorm is the beginning of the

thunderstorm.

This is taken directly from the passage, "The first stage of a thunderstorm is the cumulus, or developing stage."

6. D
The passage lists four ways that air is heated. One way is, heat created by water vapor condensing into liquid.

7. A
The sequence of events can be taken from these sentences:

As the moisture carried by the [1] air currents rises, it rapidly cools into liquid drops of water, which appear as cumulus clouds. As the water vapor condenses into liquid, it [2] releases heat, which warms the air. This in turn causes the air to become less dense than the surrounding dry air and [3] rise farther.

8. C
The purpose of this text is to explain when meteorologists consider a thunderstorm severe.

The main idea is the first sentence, "The United States National Weather Service classifies thunderstorms as severe when they reach a predetermined level." After the first sentence, the passage explains and elaborates on this idea. Everything is this passage is related to this idea, and there are no other major ideas in this passage that are central to the whole passage.

9. A
From this passage, we can infer that different areas and countries have different criteria for determining a severe storm.

From the passage we can see that most of the US has a criteria of, winds over 50 knots (58 mph or 93 km/h), and hail ¾ inch (2 cm). For the Central US, hail must be 1 inch (2.5 cm) in diameter. In Canada, winds must be 90 km/h or greater, hail 2 centimeters in diameter or greater, and rainfall more than 50 millimeters in 1 hour, or 75 millimeters in 3 hours.

Choice D is incorrect because the Canadian system is the same for hail, 2 centimeters in diameter.

10. C
With hail above the minimum size of 2.5 cm. diameter, the Central Region of the United States National Weather Service would issue a severe thunderstorm warning.

11. D
Clouds in space are made of different materials attracted by gravity. Clouds on Earth are made of water droplets or ice crystals.

Choice D is the best answer. Notice also that Choice D is the most specific.

12. C
The main idea is the first sentence of the passage; a cloud is a visible mass of droplets or frozen crystals floating in the atmosphere above the surface of the Earth or other planetary body.

The main idea is very often the first sentence of the paragraph.

13. C
This question asks about the process, and gives choices that can be confirmed or eliminated easily.

From the passage, "Dense, deep clouds reflect most light, so they appear white, at least from the top. Cloud droplets scatter light very efficiently, so the farther into a cloud light travels, the weaker it gets. This accounts for the gray or dark appearance at the base of large clouds."

We can eliminate choice A, since water droplets inside the cloud do not reflect light is false.

We can eliminate choice B, since, water droplets outside the cloud reflect light, it appears dark, is false.

Choice C is correct.

14. B
The general tone is informal.

15. B
The statement, " Fewer people have aquariums in their office than at home," cannot be inferred from this article.

16. C
The author does not provide evidence for this statement.

17. B
The following statement is an opinion, " Aquarium gravel improves the aesthetics of the aquarium."

18. D
This question tests the reader's summarization skills. The question is asking very generally about the message of the passage, and the title, "Ways Characters Communicate in Theater," is one indication of that. The other choices, A, B, and C are all directly from the text, and therefore readers may be inclined to select one of them, but are too specific to encapsulate the entirety of the passage and its message.

19. B
The paragraph on soliloquies mentions "To be or not to be," and it is from the context of that paragraph that readers may understand that because "To be or not to be" is a soliloquy, Hamlet will be introspective, or thoughtful, while delivering it. It is true that actors deliver soliloquies alone, and may be "solitary" (choice A), but "thoughtful" (choice B) is more true to the overall idea of the paragraph. Readers may choose C because drama and theater can be used interchangeably and the passage mentions that soliloquies are unique to theater (and therefore drama), but this answer is not specific enough to the paragraph in question. Readers may pick up on the theme of life and death and Hamlet's true intentions and select that he is "hopeless" (choice D), but those themes are not discussed either by this paragraph or passage, as a close textual reading and analysis confirms.

20. C

This question tests the reader's grammatical skills. Choice B seems logical, but parenthesis are actually considered to be a stronger break in a sentence than commas are, and along this line of thinking, actually disrupt the sentence more.

Choices A and D make comparisons between theater and film that are simply not made in the passage, and may or may not be true. This detail does clarify the statement that asides are most unique to theater by adding that it is not completely unique to theater, which may have been why the author didn't chose not to delete it and instead used parentheses to designate the detail's importance (choice C).

21. B

Choice A is incorrect as the Monster killed Frankenstein, not the other way around. Choice B is correct, Frankenstein is dead. Choice C is incorrect - Mary Shelley is the author. Choice D is incorrect, the person is called Frankenstein.

22. C

the speaker 'suspended" from following through on his duty to destroy the monster due to curiosity and compassion. The other choices may seem reasonable, but are not explicitly given in the passage.

23. D

All of the choices are correct.   Frankenstein's monster destroys Frankenstein by

    a. By killing Frankenstein

    b. By letting himself be the monster everyone sees him as

    c. By destroying everything Frankenstein loved

24. A

Superfluous means unnecessary.   Looking at the context of the word as it is used in the passage:

"Your repentance," I said, "is now superfluous. If you had listened to the voice of conscience and heeded the stings of remorse before you had urged your diabolical vengeance to this extremity, Frankenstein would yet have lived."

25. C
Wind is the highest source of renewable energy in Scotland. The other choices are either not mentioned at all or not mentioned in the context for how fast they are growing.

26. A
Most Scottish citizens agree with the Government's plan due to the concern for current and future needs. Choice B is a good choice but not why the majority agree. Choice C is meant to mislead the as they are clearly in sight. Choice D is a good 'common sense' choice but mentioned specifically in the text.

27. C
The up-front cost is expensive.
The other choices may appear to be correct, and even be common sense, but they are not specifically mentioned in the paragraph.

28. D
The best way to describe the paragraphs description of wind energy is clean and renewable but fluctuating.
The other choices are good descriptions of wind energy, but not the best way to describe the article.

29. A
Secede means to break away from because the 11 states wanted to leave the United States and form their own country. Choice B is incorrect because the states were not accomplishing anything   Choice C is incorrect because the states were trying to leave the USA not join it. Choice D is incorrect because the states seceded before they lost the war.

30. B
Look at the dates in the passage. The shots were fired on April 12 and Congress declared war on April 14. Choice A is incorrect because the dates show clearly which happened first. Choice C is incorrect because the passage states that Lincoln was against slavery. Choice D is incorrect because it never mentions who was or was not at Fort Sumter.

Mathematics

1. C
243/3 x 3 x 3 = 243/27 = 9

2. B
4y + 24 = 3y + 30, = 4y − 3y + 24 = 30, = y + 24 = 30, = y = 30 − 24, = y = 6

3. B
$(x^2 - y^2) / (x - y) = x + y$

$\dfrac{-(x^2 - xy)}{xy - y^2}$

$\dfrac{-(xy - y^2)}{0}$

4. A
10 x 10 x 100 x 100 = 1000^x, =100 x 10,000 = 1000^x, = 1,000,000 = 1000^x = x = 2

5. C
We are asked to find A + B - C. By paying attention to the sign distribution; we write the polynomials and operate:

A + B - C = $(-2x^4 + x^2 - 3x) + (x^4 - x^3 + 5) - (x^4 + 2x^3 + 4x + 5)$

= $-2x^4 + x^2 - 3x + x^4 - x^3 + 5 - x^4 - 2x^3 - 4x - 5$

= $-2x^4 + x^4 - x^4 - x^3 - 2x^3 + x^2 - 3x - 4x + 5 - 5$ ... similar terms written together to ease summing/substituting.

= $-2x^4 - 3x^3 + x^2 - 7x$

6. C
To find the solution for the inequality, we need to simplify it first:

$(x - 6)^2 \geq x^2 + 12$ ... we can write the open form of the left side:

$x^2 - 12x + 36 \geq x^2 + 12$ ... x^2 terms on both sides cancel each other:

$-12x + 36 \geq 12$ ... Now, we aim to have x alone on one side.

So, we subtract 36 from both sides:

-12x + 36 - 36 ≥ 12 - 36

-12x ≥ -24 ... We divide both sides by -12. This means that the inequality will change its direction:

x ≤ 2 ... x can be 2 or a smaller value.

This result is shown by (-∞, 2].

7. B
$(7 \times 7 \times 7 \times 7 \times 7) - (3 \times 3 \times 3 \times 3 \times 3) = 16,807 - 243 = 16,564$.

8. C
$(x^3 - 3x^2 + 3x - 1) / (x - 1) = x^2 - 2x + 1$
$\underline{-(x^3 - x^2)}$
$\qquad -2x^2 + 3x - 1$
$\quad \underline{-(-2\ x^2 + 2x)}$
$\qquad\qquad x - 1$

$\underline{-(x - 1)}$
0

9. C
Exponential form is 9^3 and standard from is 729

10. B
$x^2 - 5x - 6 = 0$

We try to separate the middle term -5x to find common factors with x^2 and -6 separately:

$x^2 - 6x + x - 6 = 0$ ... Here, we see that x is a common factor for x^2 and -6x:

$x(x - 6) + x - 6 = 0$ ... Here, we have x times x - 6 and 1 time x - 6 summed up. This means that we have x + 1 times x - 6:

$(x + 1)(x - 6) = 0$ ... This is true when either or both of the expressions in the parenthesis are equal to zero:

$x + 1 = 0$ ... $x = -1$

$x - 6 = 0$ ... $x = 6$

-1 and 6 are the solutions for this quadratic equation.

11. B
0.524/ (10•10•10) = 0.524/1000 ... This means that we need to carry the decimal point 3 decimals left from the point it is now:

= 0.0.0.0.524 = 0.000524

12. A
We need to find the greatest common divisor of the two terms in order to factor the expression. We should remember that if the bases of exponent numbers are the same, the multiplication of two terms is found by summing the powers and writing on the same base. Similarly; when dividing, the power of the divisor is subtracted from the power of the divided.
Both x^3y^3 and x^2y^8 contain x^2 and y^3. So;

$x^3y^3 - x^2y^8 = x•x^2y^3 - y^5•x^2y^3$ ... We can carry x^2y^3 out as the factor:

$= x^2y^3(x - y^5)$

13. D
Our aim is to collect the knowns on one side, and the unknowns (x terms) on the other side:

$5x/2 = (3x + 24)/6$ ... First, we can simplify the denominators of both sides by 2:

$5x = (3x + 24)/3$ ... Now, we can do cross multiplication:

$15x = 3x + 24$

$15x - 3x = 24$

$12x = 24$

$x = 24/12 = 2$

14. D
When multiplying exponents with the same base, add the

exponents. $3^2 \times 3^5 = 3^{2+5} = 3^7$

15. C
Solving the system means finding x and y. Since we also have a in the system, we will find x and y depending on a.

We can obtain y by using the equation ax + y = 1:

y = 1 - ax ... Then, we can insert this value into the second equation:

x + a(1 - ax) = 1

$x + a - a^2x = 1$

$x - a^2x = 1 - a$

$x(1 - a^2) = 1 - a$ ... We need to obtain x alone:

$x = (1 - a)/(1 - a^2)$ ... Here, $1 - a^2 = (1 - a)(1 + a)$ is used:

x = (1 - a)/((1 - a)(1 + a)) ... Simplifying by (1 - a):

x = 1/(a + 1) ... Now we know the value of x. By using either of the equations, we can find the value of y. Let us use y = 1 - ax:

y = 1 - a•1/(a + 1)

y = 1 - a/(a + 1) ... By writing on the same denominator:

y = ((a + 1) - a)/(a + 1)

y = (a + 1 - a)/(a + 1) ... a and -a cancel each other:

y = 1/(a + 1) ... x and y are found to be equal.

The solution of the system is (1/(a + 1), 1/(a + 1))

16. A
To divide exponents with the same base, subtract the exponents. $3^{8-5} = 3^3$

17. C
To solve the linear equation, we operate the knowns and unknowns within each other and try to obtain x term (which is the unknown) alone on one side of the equation:

3(x + 2) - 2(1 - x) = 4x + 5 ... We remove the parenthesis by distributing the factors:

$3x + 6 - 2 + 2x = 4x + 5$

$5x + 4 = 4x + 5$

$5x - 4x = 5 - 4$

$x = 1$

18. C
$3x^a + 6a^x - x^a + (-5a^x) - 2x^a = 3x^a + 6a^x - x^a - 5a^x - 2x^a = a^x$

19. B
By paying attention to the sign distribution; we write the polynomials and operate:
$(-3x^2 + 2x + 6) + (-x^2 - x - 1)$

$= -3x^2 + 2x + 6 - x^2 - x - 1$

$= -3x^2 - x^2 + 2x - x + 6 - 1 \ldots$ similar terms written together to ease summing/substituting.

$= -4x^2 + x + 5$

20. A
10^4 is not equal to 100,000
$10^4 = 10 \times 10 \times 10 \times 10 = 10^2 \times 10^2 = 10,000$

21. D
Comparing angles on similar triangles, a, b and c will be 70°, 35°, 35°

22. A
Yes the triangles are congruent.

23. D
Perimeter of triangle ABC is asked.
Perimeter of a triangle = sum of all three sides.

Here, Perimeter of $\triangle ABC = |AC| + |CB| + |AB|$.

Since the triangle is located in the middle of two adjacent and identical rectangles, we find the side lengths using these rectangles:

$|AB| = 6 + 6 = 12$ cm

|CB| = 8.5 cm

|AC| = |CB| = 8.5 cm

Perimeter = |AC| + |CB| + |AB| = 8.5 + 8.5 + 12 = 29 cm

24. A

First, we need to simplify the value of angle a:

$a = 3\pi/2 - \pi/6 - \pi - \pi/3$ ... by equating the denominators at 6:

$a = 9\pi/6 - \pi/6 - 6\pi/6 - 2\pi/6$

$a = (9 - 1 - 6 - 2)\pi/6$

$a = 0 \cdot \pi /6$

$a = 0$

$\sin a = \sin 0° = 0$

25. A

The wheel travels $2\pi r$ distance when it makes one revolution. Here, r stands for the radius. The radius is given as 25 cm in the figure. So,
$2\pi r = 2\pi \cdot 25 = 50\pi$ cm is the distance travelled in one revolution.

In 175 revolutions: $175 \cdot 50\pi = 8750\pi$ cm is travelled.

We are asked to find the distance in meter.

1 m = 100 cm So;

8750π cm $= 8750\pi / 100 = 87.5\pi$ m

26. A

If a line represents an equation, all points on that line should satisfy the equation. Meaning that all (x, y) pairs present on the line should be able to verify that $2y - x$ is equal to 4. We can find out the correct line by trying a (x, y) point existing on each line. It is easier to choose points on the intersection of the gridlines:
Let us try the point (4, 4) on line A:

$2 \cdot 4 - 4 = 4$

$8 - 4 = 4$

$4 = 4$ ... this is a correct result, so the equation for line A is $2y - x = 4$.

Let us try other points to check the other lines:

Point (-1, 2) on line B:

$2 \cdot 2 - (-1) = 4$

$4 + 1 = 4$

$5 = 4$ ... this is a wrong result, so the equation for line B is not $2y - x = 4$.

Point (3, -1) on line C:

$2 \cdot (-1) - 3 = 4$

$-2 - 3 = 4$

$-5 = 4$ ... this is a wrong result, so the equation for line C is not $2y - x = 4$.

Point (-2, -1) on line D:

$2 \cdot (-1) - (-2) = 4$

$-2 + 2 = 4$

$0 = 4$ ... this is a wrong result, so the equation for line D is not $2y - x = 4$.

27. C

In a right angle, Pythagorean Theorem is applicable: $a^2 + b^2 = c^2$ ... Here, a and b represent the adjacent and opposite sides, c represents the hypotenuse. Hypotenuse is larger than the other two sides.

In this question, we need to try each answer choice by applying $a^2 + b^2 = c^2$ to see if it is satisfied; by inserting the largest number into c:

a. 1, 2, 3:

$1^2 + 2^2 = 3^2$

$1 + 4 = 9$

5 = 9 ... This is not correct, so answer choice does not represent a right angle whose sides are consecutive numbers.

b. 2, 3, 4:

$2^2 + 3^2 = 4^2$

$4 + 9 = 16$

13 = 16 ... This is not correct, so this answer choice does not represent a right angle whose sides are consecutive numbers.

c. 3, 4, 5:

$3^2 + 4^2 = 5^2$

$9 + 16 = 25$

25 = 25 ... This is correct, 3, 4, 5 are also consecutive numbers; so this answer choice represents a right angle whose sides are consecutive numbers.

d. 4, 5, 6:

$4^2 + 5^2 = 6^2$

$16 + 25 = 36$

41 = 36 ... This is not correct, so this answer choice does not represent a right angle whose sides are consecutive numbers.

28. A
If we call one side of the square "a," the area of the square will be a^2.

We know that $a^2 = 200$ cm^2.

On the other hand; there is an isosceles right triangle.
Pythagorean Theorem:
(Hypotenuse)^2 = (Perpendicular)^2 + (Base)^2
$h^2 = a^2 + b^2$

Given: $h^2 = 200$, $a = b = x$
Then, $x^2 + x^2 = 200$, $2x^2 = 200$, $x^2 = 100$
$x = 10$

29. B
In the question, we have a right triangle formed inside the
circle. We are asked to find the length of the hypotenuse of
this triangle. We can find the other two sides of the triangle
by using circle properties:

The diameter of the circle is equal to 12 cm. The legs of the
right triangle are the radii of the circle; so they are 6 cm
long.

Pythagorean Theorem:
(Hypotenuse)^2 = (Perpendicular)^2 + (Base)^2
$h^2 = a^2 + b^2$

Given: d (diameter)= 12 & r (radius) = $a = b = 6$
$h^2 = a^2 + b^2$
$h^2 = 6^2 + 6^2$, $h^2 = 36 + 36$
$h^2 = 72$
$h = 8.46$

30. C
Slope (m) = change in y
             change in x

$(x_1, y_1) = (-3,1)$ & $(x_2, y_2) = (1,-4)$
Slope = $[-4 - 1]/[1-(-3)] = -5/4$

Writing

1. A
Sentence 1 is least relevant, "Alvin Lee began playing guitar
at an early age, and was influenced by his parents' passion

for music and inspired by the likes of Chuck Berry and Scotty Moore."

This sentence talks about Lee's motivation rather than his achievements, which is the main topic of the paragraph. Other sentences are related to a significant extent, but this sentence deviates from the main idea the most.

2. A
Sentence 1 is the least relevant. "Curiosity was launched in late November 2011 from Cape Canaveral Air Force Station in Florida."

This paragraph talks about the objectives of the rover. All sentences other than sentence 2 mention the objectives. This sentence, however, informs us when the spacecraft was launched.

3. B
Here is the passage with the oldest to youngest trees

The earliest trees were [1] tree ferns and horsetails, which grew in forests in the Carboniferous period. Tree ferns still survive, but the only surviving horsetails are no longer in tree form. Later, in the Triassic period, [2] conifers and ginkgos, appeared, [3] followed by flowering plants after that in the Cretaceous period

4. B
The sentence refers to a person, so "who" is the only correct choice.

5. A
The sentence requires the past perfect "has always been known." The clue to this tense is the use of "since."

6. B
The superlative, "hottest," is used when expressing a temperature greater than that of anything to which it is being compared.

7. C
When comparing two items, use "the taller." When comparing more than two items, use "the tallest."

8. B
The past perfect form is used to describe an event that occurred in the past and before another event.

9. A
The subject is "rules" so the present tense plural form, "are," is used to agree with "realize."

10. C
The simple past tense, "had," is correct because it refers to completed action in the past.

11. B
The simple past tense, "sank," is correct because it refers to completed action in the past.

12. C
Among vs. Between. 'Among' is for more than 2 items, and 'between' is only for 2 items.

When he's among friends (many or more than 2), Robert seems confident, but, between you and me (two), he is very shy.

13. B
Further vs. Farther. 'Farther' is used for physical distance, and 'further' is used for figurative distance.

14. A
The verb "lay" should always take an object. Here the subject is the table. The three forms of the verb lay are: lay, laid and laid. The sentence above is in past tense.

15. B
Use the singular verb form when nouns are qualified with "every" or "each," even if they are joined by 'and. '

16. B
Use a plural verb for nouns like measles, tongs, trousers, riches, scissors etc.

17. B
Use "could," the past tense of "can" to express ability or capacity.

18. C
Comma separate phrases.

19. D
The comma separates clauses and numbers are separated with a comma. The correct sentence is,
'To travel around the globe, you have to drive 25,000 miles.'

20. A
The dog loved chasing bones, but never ate them; it was running that he enjoyed.

21. A
When using 'however,' place a comma before and after, except when however begins the sentence.

22. C
Words such as neither, each, many, either, every, everyone, everybody and any should take a singular pronoun.

23. A
The verb "ought" can be used to express desirability, duty and probability. The verb is usually followed by "to."

24. A
When two subjects are linked with "with" or "as well," use the verb form that matches the first subject.

25. A
When you use 'each other' it should be used for two things or people. When you use 'one another' it should be used for things and people above two

26. B
The verb rise ('to go up', 'to ascend.') can appear in three forms, rise, rose, and risen. The verb should not take an object.

27. A
The sentence is correct. Use "whom" in the objective case, and use "who" a subjective case.

28. B

Use a singular verb with a proper noun in plural form that refers to a single entity. Here, the The World Health Organization is a single entity, although it is made up on many members.

29. A

Will is used in the second or third person (they, he, she and you), while shall is used in the first person (I and we). Both verbs are used to express futurity.

30. A

Sentence A continues directly the discussion about tectonic plates. The other choices diverge from this central idea.

Practice Test Questions Set 2

The questions below are not the same as you will find on the PERT - that would be too easy! And nobody knows what the questions will be and they change all the time. Below are general questions that cover the same subject areas as the PERT. So, while the format and exact wording of the questions may differ slightly, and change from year to year, if you can answer the questions below, you will have no problem with the PERT.

For the best results, take these practice test questions as if it were the real exam. Set aside time when you will not be disturbed, and a location that is quiet and free of distractions. Read the instructions carefully, read each question carefully, and answer to the best of your ability.
Use the bubble answer sheets provided. When you have completed the Practice Questions, check your answer against the Answer Key and read the explanation provided.

Do not attempt more than one set of practice test questions in one day. After completing the first practice test, wait two or three days before attempting the second set of questions.

Reading Answer Sheet

1. Ⓐ Ⓑ Ⓒ Ⓓ   11. Ⓐ Ⓑ Ⓒ Ⓓ   21. Ⓐ Ⓑ Ⓒ Ⓓ

2. Ⓐ Ⓑ Ⓒ Ⓓ   12. Ⓐ Ⓑ Ⓒ Ⓓ   22. Ⓐ Ⓑ Ⓒ Ⓓ

3. Ⓐ Ⓑ Ⓒ Ⓓ   13. Ⓐ Ⓑ Ⓒ Ⓓ   23. Ⓐ Ⓑ Ⓒ Ⓓ

4. Ⓐ Ⓑ Ⓒ Ⓓ   14. Ⓐ Ⓑ Ⓒ Ⓓ   24. Ⓐ Ⓑ Ⓒ Ⓓ

5. Ⓐ Ⓑ Ⓒ Ⓓ   15. Ⓐ Ⓑ Ⓒ Ⓓ   25. Ⓐ Ⓑ Ⓒ Ⓓ

6. Ⓐ Ⓑ Ⓒ Ⓓ   16. Ⓐ Ⓑ Ⓒ Ⓓ   26. Ⓐ Ⓑ Ⓒ Ⓓ

7. Ⓐ Ⓑ Ⓒ Ⓓ   17. Ⓐ Ⓑ Ⓒ Ⓓ   27. Ⓐ Ⓑ Ⓒ Ⓓ

8. Ⓐ Ⓑ Ⓒ Ⓓ   18. Ⓐ Ⓑ Ⓒ Ⓓ   28. Ⓐ Ⓑ Ⓒ Ⓓ

9. Ⓐ Ⓑ Ⓒ Ⓓ   19. Ⓐ Ⓑ Ⓒ Ⓓ   29. Ⓐ Ⓑ Ⓒ Ⓓ

10. Ⓐ Ⓑ Ⓒ Ⓓ   20. Ⓐ Ⓑ Ⓒ Ⓓ   30. Ⓐ Ⓑ Ⓒ Ⓓ

Mathematics Answer Sheet

1. (A) (B) (C) (D)   11. (A) (B) (C) (D)   21. (A) (B) (C) (D)

2. (A) (B) (C) (D)   12. (A) (B) (C) (D)   22. (A) (B) (C) (D)

3. (A) (B) (C) (D)   13. (A) (B) (C) (D)   23. (A) (B) (C) (D)

4. (A) (B) (C) (D)   14. (A) (B) (C) (D)   24. (A) (B) (C) (D)

5. (A) (B) (C) (D)   15. (A) (B) (C) (D)   25. (A) (B) (C) (D)

6. (A) (B) (C) (D)   16. (A) (B) (C) (D)   26. (A) (B) (C) (D)

7. (A) (B) (C) (D)   17. (A) (B) (C) (D)   27. (A) (B) (C) (D)

8. (A) (B) (C) (D)   18. (A) (B) (C) (D)   28. (A) (B) (C) (D)

9. (A) (B) (C) (D)   19. (A) (B) (C) (D)   29. (A) (B) (C) (D)

10. (A) (B) (C) (D)   20. (A) (B) (C) (D)   30. (A) (B) (C) (D)

Writing Skills Answer Sheet

1. (A) (B) (C) (D)   11. (A) (B) (C) (D)   21. (A) (B) (C) (D)

2. (A) (B) (C) (D)   12. (A) (B) (C) (D)   22. (A) (B) (C) (D)

3. (A) (B) (C) (D)   13. (A) (B) (C) (D)   23. (A) (B) (C) (D)

4. (A) (B) (C) (D)   14. (A) (B) (C) (D)   24. (A) (B) (C) (D)

5. (A) (B) (C) (D)   15. (A) (B) (C) (D)   25. (A) (B) (C) (D)

6. (A) (B) (C) (D)   16. (A) (B) (C) (D)   26. (A) (B) (C) (D)

7. (A) (B) (C) (D)   17. (A) (B) (C) (D)   27. (A) (B) (C) (D)

8. (A) (B) (C) (D)   18. (A) (B) (C) (D)   28. (A) (B) (C) (D)

9. (A) (B) (C) (D)   19. (A) (B) (C) (D)   29. (A) (B) (C) (D)

10. (A) (B) (C) (D)   20. (A) (B) (C) (D)   30. (A) (B) (C) (D)

Part 1 – Reading and Language Arts

Questions 1 - 4 refer to the following passage.

The Respiratory System

The respiratory system's function is to allow oxygen exchange through all parts of the body. The anatomy or structure of the exchange system, and the uses of the exchanged gases, varies depending on the organism. In humans and other mammals, for example, the anatomical features of the respiratory system include airways, lungs, and the respiratory muscles. Molecules of oxygen and carbon dioxide are passively exchanged, by diffusion, between the gaseous external environment and the blood. This exchange process occurs in the alveolar region of the lungs.

Other animals, such as insects, have respiratory systems with very simple anatomical features, and in amphibians even the skin plays a vital role in gas exchange. Plants also have respiratory systems but the direction of gas exchange can be opposite to that of animals.

The respiratory system can also be divided into physiological, or functional, zones. These include the conducting zone (the region for gas transport from the outside atmosphere to just above the alveoli), the transitional zone, and the respiratory zone (the alveolar region where gas exchange occurs). [8]

1. What can we infer from the first paragraph in this passage?

   a.   Human and mammal respiratory systems are the same.

   b.   The lungs are an important part of the respiratory system.

   c.   The respiratory system varies in different mammals.

   d.   Oxygen and carbon dioxide are passive exchanged by the respiratory system.

2. What is the process by which molecules of oxygen and carbon dioxide are passively exchanged?

    a. Transfusion

    b. Affusion

    c. Diffusion

    d. Respiratory confusion

3. What organ plays an important role in gas exchange in amphibians?

    a. The skin

    b. The lungs

    c. The gills

    d. The mouth

4. What are the three physiological zones of the respiratory system?

    a. Conducting, transitional, respiratory zones

    b. Redacting, transitional, circulatory zones

    c. Conducting, circulatory, inhibiting zones

    d. Transitional, inhibiting, conducting zones

Questions 5 - 8 refer to the following passage.

Lightning

Lightning is an electrical discharge that occurs in a thunderstorm. Often you'll see it as a bright "bolt" (or streak) coming from the sky. Lightning occurs when static electricity inside clouds builds up and causes an electrical charge. What causes the static electricity? Water! Specifically, water droplets collide with ice crystals after the temperature in the cloud falls below freezing. Sometimes these collisions are small, but other times they're quite large. Large collisions cause large electrical charges, and when they're large enough, look out! The hyper-charged cloud will emit a burst of lightning. This lightning looks quite impressive. For a good reason, too: A lightning bolt's temperature gets so hot that it's sometimes five times hotter than the sun's surface. Although the lightning bolt is hot, it's also short-lived. Because of that, when a person is unfortunate enough to be struck by lightning, their odds of surviving are pretty good. Statistics show that 90% of victims survive a lightning blast. Oh, and that old saying, "Lightning never strikes twice in the same spot?" It's a myth! Many people report surviving lightning blasts three or more times. What's more, lightning strikes some skyscrapers multiple times. The other prominent feature of lightning storms is the thunder. This is caused by the super-heated air around a lightning bolt expands at the speed of sound. We hear thunder after seeing the lightning bolt because sound travels slower than the speed of light. In reality, though, both occur at the same moment. [9]

5. What can we infer from this passage?

a. An electrical discharge in the clouds causes lightning.

b. Lightning is not as hot as the temperature of the sun's surface.

c. The sound that lightning makes occurs when electricity strikes an object.

d. We hear lightning before we see it.

6. Being struck by lightning means:

a. Instant death.

b. Less than a fifty percent chance of survival.

c. A ninety percent chance of surviving the strike.

d. An eighty percent chance of survival.

7. Lightning is caused by the following:

    a. Water droplets colliding with ice crystals creating static electricity.

    b. Friction from the clouds rubbing together.

    c. Water droplets colliding.

    d. Warm and cold air mixing together.

Questions 9 - 12 refer to the following passage.

Low Blood Sugar

As the name suggest, low blood sugar is low sugar levels in the bloodstream. This can occur when you have not eaten properly and undertake strenuous activity, or, when you are very hungry. When Low blood sugar occurs regularly and is ongoing, it is a medical condition called hypoglycemia. This condition can occur in diabetics and in healthy adults.

Causes of low blood sugar can include excessive alcohol consumption, metabolic problems, stomach surgery, pancreas, liver or kidneys problems, as well as a side-effect of some medications.

Symptoms

There are different symptoms depending on the severity of the case.

Mild hypoglycemia can lead to feelings of nausea and hunger. The patient may also feel nervous, jittery and have fast heart beats. Sweaty skin, clammy and cold skin are likely symptoms.

Moderate hypoglycemia can result in a short temper, confusion, nervousness, fear and blurring of vision. The patient may feel weak and unsteady.

Severe cases of hypoglycemia can lead to seizures, coma, fainting spells, nightmares, headaches, excessive sweats and severe tiredness.

Diagnosis of low blood sugar

A doctor can diagnosis this medical condition by asking the patient questions and testing blood and urine samples. Home testing kits are available for patients to monitor blood sugar levels. It is important to see a qualified doctor though. The doctor can administer tests to ensure that will safely rule out other medical conditions that could affect blood sugar levels.

Treatment

Quick treatments include drinking or eating foods and drinks with high sugar contents. Good examples include soda, fruit juice, hard candy and raisins. Glucose energy tablets can also help. Doctors may also recommend medications and well as changes in diet and exercise routine to treat chronic low blood sugar.

9. Based on the article, which of the following is true?

  a. Low blood sugar can happen to anyone.

  b. Low blood sugar only happens to diabetics.

  c. Low blood sugar can occur even.

  d. None of the statements are true.

10. Which of the following are the author's opinion?

  a. Quick treatments include drinking or eating foods and drinks with high sugar contents.

  b. None of the statements are opinions.

  c. This condition can occur in diabetics and in healthy adults.

  d. There are different symptoms depending on the severity of the case

11. What is the author's purpose?

a. To inform

b. To persuade

c. To entertain

d. To analyze

12. Which of the following is not a detail?

a. A doctor can diagnosis this medical condition by asking the patient questions and testing.

b. A doctor will test blood and urine samples.

c. Glucose energy tablets can also help.

d. Home test kits monitor blood sugar levels.

Questions 13 - 16 refer to the following passage.

Myths, Legend and Folklore

Cultural historians draw a distinction between myth, legend and folktale simply as a way to group traditional stories. However, in many cultures, drawing a sharp line between myths and legends is not that simple. Instead of dividing their traditional stories into myths, legends, and folktales, some cultures divide them into two categories. The first category roughly corresponds to folktales, and the second is one that combines myths and legends. Similarly, we can not always separate myths from folktales. One society might consider a story true, making it a myth. Another society may believe the story is fiction, which makes it a folktale. In fact, when a myth loses its status as part of a religious system, it often takes on traits more typical of folktales, with its formerly divine characters now appearing as human heroes, giants, or fairies. Myth, legend, and folktale are only a few of the categories of traditional stories. Other categories include anecdotes and some kinds of jokes. Traditional stories, in turn, are only one category within the larger category of folklore, which also includes items such as gestures, costumes, and music. [10]

13. The main idea of this passage is

a. Myths, fables, and folktales are not the same thing, and each describes a specific type of story

b. Traditional stories can be categorized in different ways by different people

c. Cultures use myths for religious purposes, and when this is no longer true, the people forget and discard these myths

d. Myths can never become folk tales, because one is true, and the other is false

14. The terms myth and legend are

a. Categories that are synonymous with true and false

b. Categories that group traditional stories according to certain characteristics

c. Interchangeable, because both terms mean a story that is passed down from generation to generation

d. Meant to distinguish between a story that involves a hero and a cultural message and a story meant only to entertain

15. Traditional story categories not only include myths and legends, but

a. Can also include gestures, since some cultures passed these down before the written and spoken word

b. In addition, folklore refers to stories involving fables and fairy tales

c. These story categories can also include folk music and traditional dress

d. Traditional stories themselves are a part of the larger category of folklore, which may also include costumes, gestures, and music

16. This passage shows that

a. There is a distinct difference between a myth and a legend, although both are folktales

b. Myths are folktales, but folktales are not myths

c. Myths, legends, and folktales play an important part in tradition and the past, and are a rich and colorful part of history

d. Most cultures consider myths to be true

Questions 17 - 19 refer to the following passage.

How To Get A Good Nights Sleep

Sleep is just as essential for healthy living as water, air and food. Sleep allows the body to rest and replenish depleted energy levels. Sometimes we may for various reasons experience difficulty sleeping which has a serious effect on our health. Those who have prolonged sleeping problems are facing a serious medical condition and should see a qualified doctor when possible for help. Here is simple guide that can help you sleep better at night.

Try to create a natural pattern of waking up and sleeping around the same time everyday. This means avoiding going to bed too early and sleeping past your usual wake up time. Going to bed and getting up at radically different times everyday confuses your body clock. Try to establish a natural rhythm as much as you can.

Exercises and a bit of physical activity can help you sleep better at night. If you are having problem sleeping, try to be as active as you can during the day. If you are tired from physical activity, falling asleep is a natural and easy process for your body. If you remain inactive during the day, you will find it harder to sleep properly at night. Try walking, jogging, swimming or simple stretches as you get close to your bed time.

Afternoon naps are great to refresh you during the day, but

they may also keep you awake at night. If you feel sleepy during the day, get up, take a walk and get busy to keep from sleeping. Stretching is a good way to increase blood flow to the brain and keep you alert so that you don't sleep during the day. This will help you sleep better night.

> A warm bath or a glass of milk in the evening can help your body relax and prepare for sleep. A cold bath will wake you up and keep you up for several hours. Also avoid eating too late before bed.

17. How would you describe this sentence?

    a. A recommendation

    b. An opinion

    c. A fact

    d. A diagnosis

18. Which of the following is an alternative title for this article?

    a. Exercise and a good night's sleep

    b. Benefits of a good night's sleep

    c. Tips for a good night's sleep

    d. Lack of sleep is a serious medical condition

19. Which of the following can not be inferred from this article?

    a. Biking is helpful for getting a good night's sleep

    b. Mental activity is helpful for getting a good night's sleep

    c. Eating bedtime snacks is not recommended

    d. Getting up at the same time is helpful for a good night's sleep

Questions 18 - 20 refer to the following passage.

Navy SEAL

The United States Navy's Sea, Air and Land Teams, commonly known as Navy SEALs, are the U.S. Navy's principle special operations force and a part of the Naval Special Warfare Command (NSWC) as well as the maritime component of the United States Special Operations Command (USSOCOM).

The unit's acronym ("SEAL") comes from their capacity to operate at sea, in the air, and on land – but it is their ability to work underwater that separates SEALs from most other military units in the world. Navy SEALs are trained and have been deployed in a wide variety of missions, including direct action and special reconnaissance operations, unconventional warfare, foreign internal defense, hostage rescue, counter-terrorism and other missions. All SEALs are members of either the United States Navy or the United States Coast Guard.

In the early morning of 2 May 2011 local time, a team of 40 CIA-led Navy SEALs completed an operation to kill Osama bin Laden in Abbottabad, Pakistan about 35 miles (56 km) from Islamabad, the country's capital. The Navy SEALs were part of the Naval Special Warfare Development Group, previously called "Team 6." President Barack Obama later confirmed the death of bin Laden. The unprecedented media coverage raised the public profile of the SEAL community, particularly the counter-terrorism specialists commonly known as SEAL Team 6. [11]

18. Are Navy Seals part of USSOCOM?

  a. Yes.

  b. No.

  c. Only for special operations.

  d. No, they are part of the US Navy.

20. What separates Navy SEALs from other military units?

a. Belonging to NSWC.

b. Direct action and special reconnaissance operations.

c. Working underwater.

d. Working for other military units in the world.

Questions 21 - 24 refer to the following passage.

The Crusades

In 1095 Pope Urban II proclaimed the First Crusade with the intent and stated goal to restore Christian access to holy places in and around Jerusalem. Over the next 200 years there were 6 major crusades and numerous minor crusades in the fight for control of the "Holy Land." Historians are divided on the real purpose of the Crusades, some believing that it was part of a purely defensive war against Islamic conquest; some see them as part of a long-running conflict at the frontiers of Europe; and others see them as confident, aggressive, papal-led expansion attempts by Western Christendom. The impact of the crusades was profound, and judgment of the Crusaders ranges from laudatory to highly critical. However, all agree that the Crusades and wars waged during those crusades were brutal and often bloody. Several hundred thousand Roman Catholic Christians joined the Crusades, they were Christians from all over Europe.

Europe at the time was under the Feudal System, so while the Crusaders made vows to the Church they also were beholden to their Feudal Lords. This led to the Crusaders not only fighting the Saracen, the commonly used word for Muslim at the time, but also each other for power and economic gain in the Holy Land. This infighting between the Crusaders is why many historians hold the view that the Crusades were simply a front for Europe to invade the Holy Land for economic gain in the name of the Church. Another factor contributing to this theory is that while the army of crusaders marched towards Jerusalem they pillaged the land as they went. The church and feudal Lords vowing to return the land to its original beauty, and inhabitants, this rarely happened though as the Lords often kept the land for themselves. A full 800 years after the Crusades, Pope John Paul II expressed his sorrow for the massacre of innocent people and the lasting damage the Medieval church caused in that area of the World.

21. What is the tone of this article?

    a. Subjective

    b. Objective

    c. Persuasive

    d. None of the Above

22. What can all historians agree on concerning the Crusades?

    a. It achieved great things

    b. It stabilized the Holy Land

    c. It was bloody and brutal

    d. It helped defend Europe from the Byzantine Empire

23. What impact did the feudal system have on the Crusades

    a. It unified the Crusaders

    b. It helped gather volunteers

    c. It had no effect on the Crusades

    d. It led to infighting, causing more damage than good

24. What does Saracen mean?

    a. Muslim

    b. Christian

    c. Knight

    d. Holy Land

Questions 25 - 28 refer to the following two passages.

**Annabelle Lee First and Third Stanza
by Edgar Allan Poe**

It was many and many a year ago,
In a kingdom by the sea,
That a maiden there lived whom you may know
By the name of Annabel Lee;
And this maiden she lived with no other thought
Than to love and be loved by me.

But our love it was stronger by far than the love
Of those who were older than we
Of many far wiser than we
And neither the angels in heaven above,
Nor the demons down under the sea,
Can ever dissever my soul from the soul
Of the beautiful Annabel Lee.
For the moon never beams without bringing me dreams
Of the beautiful Annabel Lee;
And the stars never rise but I feel the bright eyes
Of the beautiful Annabel Lee;
And so, all the night-tide, I lie down by the side
Of my darling, my darling, my life and my bride,
In the sepulcher there by the sea,
In her tomb by the sounding sea.

Leo Tolstoy, War and Peace

"Yes, love, ...but not the love that loves for something, to
gain something, or because of something, but that love that
I felt for the first time, when dying, I saw my enemy and yet
loved him. I knew that feeling of love which is the essence
of the soul, for which no object is needed. And I know that
blissful feeling now too. To love one's neighbours; to love
one's enemies. To love everything - to Love God in all His
manifestations. Some one dear to one can be loved with human love; but an enemy can only be loved with divine love.
And that was why I felt such joy when I felt that I loved that
man. What happened to him? Is he alive? ...Loving with human love, one may pass from love to hatred; but divine love
cannot change. Nothing, not even death, can shatter it. It

is the very nature of the soul. And how many people I have
hated in my life. And of all people none I have loved and
hated more than her.... If it were only possible for me to see
her once more... once, looking into those eyes to say..."

**25. What is the difference between the two kinds of love
described in these passages?**

> a. One speaks to romantic love and the other Divine
> love
>
> b. There is no difference
>
> c. Young love, and old love
>
> d. Both a and c.

**26. In the poem, the author refers to Annabelle Lee in
the past tense, why?**

> a. Because she no longer loves him
>
> b. Because she has died
>
> c. For stylistic reasons
>
> d. None of the above

**27. Agape is Greek for "unconditional love," which pas-
sage better describes unconditional love?**

> a. The Poem by Edgar Allen Poe
>
> b. The Excerpt from War and Peace by Leo Tolstoy
>
> c. Neither passage
>
> d. Both passages

**28. The dying man in the second passage, how many
people does he specifically say he loves in the passage?**

> a. One
>
> b. Two
>
> c. Three
>
> d. Four

Questions 29 - 30 refer to the following passages.

**The Daffodils
by William Wordsworth**

I wandered lonely as a cloud
That floats on high o'er vales and hills,
When all at once I saw a crowd,
A host, of golden daffodils;
Beside the lake, beneath the trees,
Fluttering and dancing in the breeze.

Continuous as the stars that shine
And twinkle on the Milky Way,
They stretched in never-ending line
Along the margin of a bay:
Ten thousand saw I at a glance,
Tossing their heads in sprightly dance.

The waves beside them danced, but they
Out-did the sparkling waves in glee:
A Poet could not but be gay,
In such a jocund company:
I gazed--and gazed--but little thought
What wealth the show to me had brought:

For oft, when on my couch I lie
In vacant or in pensive mood,
They flash upon that inward eye
Which is the bliss of solitude;
And then my heart with pleasure fills,
And dances with the daffodils.

29. Is the author of this poem a lover of nature?

    a. Yes.

    b. No.

    c. Uncertain. There isn't enough information.

30. What is the general mood of this poem?

    a. Sad

    b. Thoughtful

    c. Happy

    d. Excited

Mathematics

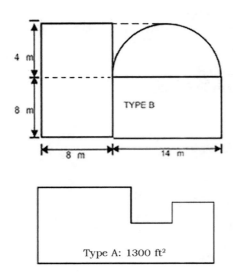

Type A: 1300 ft²

1. The price of houses in a certain subdivision is based on the total area. Susan is watching her budget and wants to choose the house with the lowest area. Which house type, A (1300 ft2) or B, should she choose if she would like the house with the lowest price? (1cm² = 4.0ft² & π = 22/7)

    a. Type B is smaller 140 ft²

    b. Type A is smaller

    c. Type B is smaller at 855 ft²

    d. Type B is larger

2. Using the quadratic formula, solve the quadratic equation: $0.9x^2 + 1.8x - 2.7 = 0$

    a. 1 and 3

    b. -3 and 1

    c. -3 and -1

    d. -1 and 3

3. Subtract polynomials $4x^3 - 2x^2 - 10$ and $5x^3 + x^2 + x + 5$.

    a. $-x^3 - 3x^2 - x - 15$

    b. $9x^3 - 3x^2 - x - 15$

    c. $-x^3 - x^2 + x - 5$

    d. $9x^3 - x^2 + x + 5$

4. Find x and y from the following system of equations:

$(4x + 5y)/3 = ((x - 3y)/2) + 4$
$(3x + y)/2 = ((2x + 7y)/3) -1$

    a. (1, 3)

    b. (2, 1)

    c. (1, 1)

    d. (0, 1)

5. Using the factoring method, solve the quadratic equation: $x^2 + 12x - 13 = 0$

    a. -13 and 1

    b. -13 and -1

    c. 1 and 13

    d. -1 and 13

6. Using the quadratic formula, solve the quadratic equation:

$$\frac{x+2}{x-2} + \frac{x-2}{x+2} = 0$$

    a. It has infinite numbers of solutions

    b. 0 and 1

    c. It has no solutions

    d. 0

7. Turn the following expression into a simple polynomial:

$5(3x^2 - 2) - x^2(2 - 3x)$

    a. $3x^3 + 17x^2 - 10$

    b. $3x^3 + 13x^2 + 10$

    c. $-3x^3 - 13x^2 - 10$

    d. $3x^3 + 13x^2 - 10$

8. Solve $(x^3 + 2)(x^2 - x) - x^5$.

    a. $2x^5 - x^4 + 2x^2 - 2x$

    b. $-x^4 + 2x^2 - 2x$

    c. $-x^4 - 2x^2 - 2x$

    d. $-x^4 + 2x^2 + 2x$

9. $9ab^2 + 8ab^2 =$

    a. ab^2

    b. $17ab^2$

    c. 17

    d. $17a^2b^2$

10. Factor the polynomial $x^2 - 7x - 30$.

    a. $(x + 15)(x - 2)$
    b. $(x + 10)(x - 3)$
    c. $(x - 10)(x + 3)$
    d. $(x - 15)(x + 2)$

11. If a and b are real numbers, solve the following equation: $(a + 2)x - b = -2 + (a + b)x$

    a. -1
    b. 0
    c. 1
    d. 2

12. If $A = -2x^4 + x^2 - 3x$, $B = x^4 - x^3 + 5$ and $C = x^4 + 2x^3 + 4x + 5$, find $A + B - C$.

    a. $x^3 + x^2 + x + 10$
    b. $-3x^3 + x^2 - 7x + 10$
    c. $-2x^4 - 3x^3 + x^2 - 7x$
    d. $-3x^4 + x^3 + x^2 - 7x$

13. $(4Y^3 - 2Y^2) + (7Y^2 + 3y - y) =$

    a. $4y^3 + 9y^2 + 4y$
    b. $5y^3 + 5y^2 + 3y$
    c. $4y^3 + 7y^2 + 2y$
    d. $4y^3 + 5y^2 + 2y$

14. Turn the following expression into a simple polynomial: $1 - x(1 - x(1 - x))$

    a. $x^3 + x^2 - x + 1$
    b. $-x^3 - x^2 + x + 1$
    c. $-x^3 + x^2 - x + 1$
    d. $x^3 + x^2 - x - 1$

15. 7(2y + 8) + 1 – 4(y + 5) =

    a. 10y + 36

    b. 10y + 77

    c. 18y + 37

    (d) 10y + 37

16. Richard gives 's' amount of salary to each of his 'n' employees weekly. If he has 'x' amount of money then how many days he can employ these 'n' employees.

    a. sx/7n

    b. 7x/nx

    c. nx/7s

    (d) 7x/ns

17. Factor the polynomial x^2 - 3x - 4.

    (a) (x + 1)(x - 4)

    b. (x - 1)(x + 4)

    c. (x - 1)(x - 4)

    d. (x + 1)(x + 4)

18. Solve the inequality: (2x + 1)/(2x - 1) < 1.

    a. (-2, + ∞)

    b. (1, + ∞)

    c. (-∞, -2)

    (d) (-∞, 1/2)

19. Using the quadratic formula, solve the quadratic equation:

$(a^2 - b^2)x^2 + 2ax + 1 = 0$

    a. $a/(a + b)$ and $b/(a + b)$

    b. $1/(a + b)$ and $a/(a + b)$

    c. $a/(a + b)$ and $a/(a - b)$

    ⓓ $-1/(a + b)$ and $-1/(a - b)$

20. Turn the following expression into a simple polynomial: (a + b) (x + y) + (a - b) (x - y) - (ax + by)

    ⓐ $ax + by$

    b. $ax - by$

    c. $ax^2 + by^2$

    d. $ax^2 - by^2$

21. Given polynomials A = $4x^5 - 2x^2 + 3x - 2$ and B = $-3x^4 - 5x^2 - 4x + 5$, find A + B.

    a. $x^5 - 3x^2 - x - 3$

    b. $4x^5 - 3x^4 + 7x^2 + x + 3$

    ⓒ $4x^5 - 3x^4 - 7x^2 - x + 3$

    d. $4x^5 - 3x^4 - 7x^2 - x - 7$

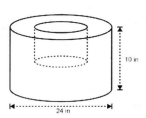

Note: figure not drawn to scale

22. What is the volume of the above solid made by a hollow cylinder that is half the size (in all dimensions) of the larger cylinder?

    a. 1440 п in³

    b. 1260 п in³

    c. 1040 п in³

    d. 960 п in³

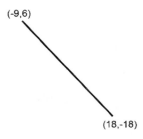

23. What is the slope of the line above?

    a. -8/9

    b. 9/8

    c. -9/8

    d. 8/9

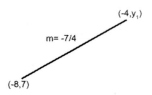

24. With the data given above, what is the value of y_1?

    a. 0

    b. -7

    c. 7

    d. 8

25. The area of a rectangle is 20 cm². If one side increases by 1 cm and other by 2 cm, the area of the new rectangle is 35 cm². Find the sides of the original rectangle.

     a. (4,8)

     b. (4,5)

     c. (2.5,8)

     d. b and c

(18,12)

(9,-6)

26. What is the distance between the two points?

     a. ≈19

     b. 22

     c. ≈21

     d. ≈20

27. Find the solution for the following linear equation:
1/(4x - 2) = 5/6

     a. 0.2

     b. 0.4

     c. 0.6

     d. 0.8

28. How much water can be stored in a cylindrical container 5 meters in diameter and 12 meters high?

Note: figure not drawn to scale

a. 235.65 m³

b. 223.65 m³

c. 240.65 m³

d. 252.65 m³

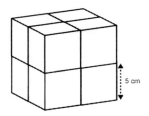

Note: figure not drawn to scale

29. Assuming the figure above is composed of cubes, what is the volume?

a. 125 cm³

b. 875 cm³

c. 1000 cm³

d. 500 cm³

30. Solve

$x \sqrt{5} - y = \sqrt{5}$
$x - y \sqrt{5} = 5$

    a. $(0, -\sqrt{5})$
    b. $(0, \sqrt{5})$
    c. $(-\sqrt{5}, 0)$
    d. $(\sqrt{5}, 0)$

Writing

Directions: Choose the word or phrase that best completes the sentence.

1. _____ won first place in the Western Division?

    a. Whom
    b. Which
    c. What
    d. Who

2. There are now several ways to listen to music, including radio, CDs, and Mp3 files _____ you can download onto an MP3 player.

    a. on which
    b. who
    c. whom
    d. which

3. As the tallest monument in the United States, the St. Louis Arch _____ to an impressive 630 feet.

    a. has rose

    b. is risen

    c. rises

    d. No change is necessary.

4. The tired, old woman should _____ on the sofa.

    a. lie

    b. lays

    c. laid

    d. None of the options are correct.

5. Did the students understand that Thanksgiving always _____ on the fourth Thursday in November?

    a None of the options are correct.

    b. falling

    c. has fell

    d. falls

6. Collecting stamps, _____ models, and listening to shortwave radio were Rick's main hobbies.

    a. building

    b. build

    c. having built

    d. None of the options are correct.

7. Every morning, after the kids _____ for school and before the sun came up, my mother makes herself a cup of cocoa.

    a. had left

    b. leave

    c. have left

    d. None of the options are correct.

8. Elaine promised to bring the camera _____ at the mall yesterday.

    a. by me

    b. with me

    c. at me

    d. to me

9. Last night, he _____ the sleeping bag down beside my mattress.

    a. lay

    b. lain

    c. has laid

    d. laid

10. I would have bought the shirt for you if _____ you liked it.

    a. had known

    b. have known

    c. would know

    d. None of the options are correct.

11. Until you _____ the overdue books to the library, you can't take any new ones home.

      a. take
      b. bring
      c. None of the choices are correct.

12. If they had gone to the party, he would _____ too.

      a. gone

      b. went

      c. have went

      d. had went

13. His doctor suggested that he eat _____ snacks and do less lounging on the couch.

      a. less

      b. fewer

      c. None of the choices are correct.

14. His father is _____.

      a. a poet and novelist

      b. a poet and a novelist

      c. either of the above

      d. none of the above

15. Choose the sentence with the correct punctuation.

      a. George wrecked John's car that was the end of their friendship.

      b. George wrecked John's car. that was the end of their friendship.

      c. The sentence is correct.

      d. None of the choices are correct.

16. Choose the sentence with the correct punctuation.

a. The dress was not Gina's favorite; however, she wore it to the dance.
b. None of the choices are correct.
c. The dress was not Gina's favorite, however; she wore it to the dance.
d. The dress was not Gina's favorite however, she wore it to the dance.

17. Choose the sentence with the correct punctuation.

a. Chris showed his dedication to golf in many ways, for example, he watched all of the tournaments on television.

b. The sentence is correct.

c. Chris showed his dedication to golf in many ways, for example; he watched all of the tournaments on television.

d. Chris showed his dedication to golf in many ways for example he watched all of the tournaments on television.

18. Choose the sentence with the correct grammar.

a. If Joe had told me the truth, I wouldn't have been so angry.
b. If Joe would have told me the truth, I wouldn't have been so angry.
c. I wouldn't have been so angry if Joe would have told the truth.
d. If Joe would have telled me the truth, I wouldn't have been so angry.

19. Choose the sentence with the correct punctuation.

a. I can never remember how to use those two common words, "sell," meaning to trade a product for money, or sale- meaning an event where products are traded for less money than usual.

b. I can never remember how to use those two common words, "sell," meaning to trade a product for money, or "sale," meaning an event where products are traded for less money than usual.

c. I can never remember how to use those two common words, "sell," meaning to trade a product for money, or sale, meaning an event where products are traded for less money than usual.

d. None of the above are correct.

20. Choose the sentence with the correct punctuation.

a. The class just finished reading, -"Leinengen versus the Ants," a short story by Carl Stephenson about a plantation owner's battle with army ants.

b. The class just finished reading, Leinengen versus the Ants, a short story by Carl Stephenson about a plantation owner's battle with army ants.

c. The class just finished reading, "Leinengen versus the Ants," a short story by Carl Stephenson about a plantation owner's battle with army ants.

d. None of the above

21. Choose the sentence with the correct punctuation.

a. My best friend said, "always count your change."

b. My best friend said, "<u>Always Count your Change</u>."

c. My best friend said, "Always count your change."

d. None of the choices are correct.

22. Choose the sentence that is written correctly.

a. He told him to rise it up

b. He told him to raise it up

c. Either of the above

d. None of the above

23. Choose the sentence that is written correctly.

a. I shall arrive early and I will have breakfast with you

b. I shall arrive early and I would have breakfast with you

c. I shall arrive early and have breakfast with you.

d. None of the above

24. Choose the sentence that is written correctly.

a. The gold coins with the diamonds is to be seized

b. The gold coins with the diamonds are to be seized.

c. None of the above

25. Choose the sentence that is written correctly.

a The trousers are to be delivered today

b. The trousers is to be delivered today.

c. Both of the above

26. Choose the sentence that is written correctly.

a. She was nodding her head, her hips are swaying.

b. She was nodding her head, her hips is swaying.

c. She was nodding her head, her hips were swaying.

d. None of the above

27. Choose the sentence that is written correctly.

a. The sad news were delivered this morning

b. The sad news are delivered this morning.

c. The sad news was delivered this morning

d. None of the above

28. Choose the sentence that is written correctly.

a. The sentence is correct

b. Mathematics are my best subject in school

c. Mathematics was my best subject in school

d. Mathematics were my best subject in school.

29. Choose the sentence that is written correctly.

a. 15 minutes is all the time you have to complete the test.

b. 15 minutes are all the time you have to complete the test.

c. Both of the above.

d. None of the above.

30. Choose the sentence that is written correctly.

a. Everyone are to wear a black tie.

b. Everyone have to wear a black tie.

c. Everyone has to wear a black tie.

d. None of the above.

Answer Key

Reading Comprehension

1. B
We can infer an important part of the respiratory system are the lungs. From the passage, "Molecules of oxygen and carbon dioxide are passively exchanged, by diffusion, between the gaseous external environment and the blood. This exchange process occurs in the alveolar region of the lungs." Therefore, one of the primary functions for the respiratory system is the exchange of oxygen and carbon dioxide, and this process occurs in the lungs. We can therefore infer that the lungs are an important part of the respiratory system.

2. C
The process by which molecules of oxygen and carbon dioxide are passively exchanged is diffusion.
This is a definition type question. Scan the passage for references to "oxygen," "carbon dioxide," or "exchanged."

3. A
The organ that plays an important role in gas exchange in amphibians is the skin.
Scan the passage for references to "amphibians," and find the answer.

4. A
The three physiological zones of the respiratory system are Conducting, transitional, respiratory zones.

5. A
We can infer that, an electrical discharge in the clouds causes lightning.

The passage tells us that, "Lightning occurs when static electricity inside clouds builds up and causes an electrical charge,"

6. C
Being struck by lightning means, a ninety percent chance of

surviving the strike.

From the passage, "statistics show that 90% of victims survive a lightning blast."

7. A
We know that lightning is static electricity from the third sentence in the passage. We also know that water droplets colliding with ice crystals cause static electricity. Therefore, Lightning is caused by water droplets colliding with ice crystals.

8. A
Low blood sugar occurs both in diabetics and healthy adults.

9. B
None of the statements are the author's opinion.

10. A
The author's purpose is the inform.

11. A
The only statement that is not a detail is, "A doctor can diagnosis this medical condition by asking the patient questions and testing."

12. B
This passage describes the different categories for traditional stories. The other choices are facts from the passage, not the main idea of the passage. The main idea of a passage will always be the most general statement. For example, choice A, Myths, fables, and folktales are not the same thing, and each describes a specific type of story. This is a true statement from the passage, but not the main idea of the passage, since the passage also talks about how some cultures may classify a story as a myth and others as a folktale. The statement, from choice B, Traditional stories can be categorized in different ways by different people, is a more general statement that describes the passage.

13. B
Choice B is the best choice, categories that group traditional stories according to certain characteristics.

Choices A and C are false and can be eliminated right away. Choice D is designed to confuse. Choice D may be true, but it is not mentioned in the passage.

14. D
The best answer is D, traditional stories themselves are a part of the larger category of folklore, which may also include costumes, gestures, and music.

All the other choices are false. Traditional stories are part of the larger category of Folklore, which includes other things, not the other way around.

15. A
The sentence is a recommendation.

16. C
Tips for a good night's sleep is the best alternative title for this article.

17. B
Mental activity is helpful for a good night's sleep is can not be inferred from this article.

18. C
This question tests the reader's vocabulary and contextualization skills. Choice A may or may not be true, but focuses on the wrong function of the word "give" and ignores the rest of the sentence, which is more relevant to what the passage is discussing. Choices B and D may also be selected if the reader depends too literally on the word "give," failing to grasp the more abstract function of the word that is the focus of choice C, which also properly acknowledges the entirety of the passage and its meaning.

19. A
Navy Seals are the maritime component of the United States Special Operations Command (USSOCOM).

20. C
Working underwater separates SEALs from other military units. This is taken directly from the passage.

21. A
Choice B is incorrect; the author did not express their opinion on the subject matter. Choice C is incorrect, the author was not trying to prove a point.

22. C
Choice C is correct; historians believe it was brutal and bloody. Choice A is incorrect; there is no consensus that the Crusades achieved great things. Choice B is incorrect; it did not stabilize the Holy Lands. Choice D is incorrect, some historians do believe this was the purpose but not all historians.

23. D
The feudal system led to infighting. Choice A is incorrect, it had the opposite effect. Choice B is incorrect, though this is a good answer, it is not the best answer. The Church asked for volunteers not the Feudal Lords. Choice C is incorrect, it did have an effect on the Crusades.

24. A
Saracen was a generic term for Muslims widely used in Europe during the later medieval era.

25. A
The first speaks to romantic love, a boy has for Annabelle Lee, the second divine love. Choice B is incorrect for the same reason - both passages speak of different types of love. Choice C is incorrect. While the first passage alludes to young love the second passage makes no distinction.

26. B
A careful reading will show in the last line, she is in a tomb, meaning she has died. Choice A is incorrect. While this could be correct, it is not the best and most accurate answer, because she has died. Choice C is incorrect because the past tense is used for a specific reason and has nothing to do with style.

27. B
Divine love is unchanging and therefore unconditional. Choice A is incorrect since romantic love can be conditional. Choice C is incorrect, the second passage is correct. Choice

D is incorrect, the first passage is incorrect.

28. C
He loves three people, the man, his enemy, and the un-named woman.

29. A
The author is enjoying the daffodils very much, so we can infer that he is a lover of nature.

30. C
The mood of this poem is happy.   From the last line,

> And then my heart with pleasure fills,
> And dances with the daffodils.

Mathematics

1. D
Area of Type B consists of two rectangles and a half circle. We can find these three areas and sum them up in order to find the total area:

Area of the left rectangle: $(4 + 8) \cdot 8 = 96$ m^2

Area of the right rectangle: $14 \cdot 8 = 112$ m^2

The diameter of the circle is equal to 14 m. So, the radius is $14/2 = 7$:

Area of the half circle = $(1/2) \cdot \pi r^2 = (1/2) \cdot (22/7) \cdot (7)^2 = (1 \cdot 22 \cdot 49)/(2 \cdot 7) = 77$ m^2

Area of Type B = $96 + 112 + 77 = 285$ m^2

Converting this area to ft^2: 285 m^2 = $285 \cdot 10.76$ ft^2 = 3066.6 ft^2

Type B is (3066.6 - 1300 = 1766.6 ft^2) 1766.6 ft^2 larger than type A.

2. B
To solve the equation, we need the equation in the form $ax^2 + bx + c = 0$.

$0.9x^2 + 1.8x - 2.7 = 0$ is already in this form.

The quadratic formula to find the roots of a quadratic equation is:

$x_{1,2} = (-b \pm \sqrt{\Delta}) / 2a$ where $\Delta = b^2 - 4ac$ and is called the discriminant of the quadratic equation.

In our question, the equation is $0.9x^2 + 1.8x - 2.7 = 0$. To eliminate the decimals, let us multiply the equation by 10:

$9x^2 + 18x - 27 = 0$ ... This equation can be simplified by 9 since each term contains 9:

$x^2 + 2x - 3 = 0$

By remembering the form $ax^2 + bx + c = 0$:

$a = 1, b = 2, c = -3$

So, we can find the discriminant first, and then the roots of the equation:

$\Delta = b^2 - 4ac = (2)^2 - 4 \cdot 1 \cdot (-3) = 4 + 12 = 16$

$x_{1,2} = (-b \pm \sqrt{\Delta}) / 2a = (-2 \pm \sqrt{16}) / 2 = (-2 \pm 4) / 2$

This means that the roots are,

$x_1 = (-2 - 4)/2 = -3$ and $x_2 = (-2 + 4)/2 = 1$

4. C
First, we need to arrange the two equations to obtain the form $ax + by = c$. We see that there are 3 and 2 in the denominators of both equations. If we equate all at 6, then we can cancel all 6 in the denominators and have straight equations:

Equate all denominators at 6:

$2(4x + 5y)/6 = 3(x - 3y)/6 + 4 \cdot 6/6$ ... Now we can cancel 6 in the denominators:

$8x + 10y = 3x - 9y + 24$ ... We can collect x and y terms on left side of the equation:

8x + 10y - 3x + 9y = 24

5x + 19y = 24 ... Equation (I)

Let us arrange the second equation:

3(3x + y)/6 = 2(2x + 7y)/6 - 1•6/6 ... Now we can cancel 6 in the denominators:

9x + 3y = 4x + 14y - 6 ... We can collect x and y terms on left side of the equation:

9x + 3y - 4x - 14y = -6

5x - 11y = -6 ... Equation (II)

Now, we have two equations and two unknowns x and y. By writing the two equations one under the other and operating, we can find one unknowns first, and find the other next:

   5x + 19y = 24

-1/ 5x - 11y = -6 ... If we substitute this equation from the upper one, 5x cancels -5x:

   5x + 19y = 24

   -5x + 11y = 6 ... Summing side-by-side:

5x - 5x + 19y + 11y = 24 + 6

30y = 30 ... Dividing both sides by 30:

y = 1

Inserting y = 1 into either of the equations, we can find the value of x. Choosing equation I:

5x + 19•1 = 24

5x = 24 - 19

5x = 5 ... Dividing both sides by 5:

x = 1

So, x = 1 and y = 1 is the solution; it is shown as (1, 1).

5. A

x^2 + 12x - 13 = 0 ... We try to separate the middle term 12x to find common factors with x^2 and -13 separately:

x^2 + 13x - x - 13 = 0 ... Here, we see that x is a common factor for x^2 and 13x, and -1 is a common factor for -x and -13:

x(x + 13) - 1(x + 13) = 0 ... Here, we have x times x + 13 and -1 times x + 13 summed up. This means that we have x - 1 times x + 13:

(x - 1)(x + 13) = 0

This is true when either or, both of the expressions in the parenthesis are equal to zero:

x - 1 = 0 ... x = 1

x + 13 = 0 ... x = -13

1 and -13 are the solutions for this quadratic equation.

6. C

This equation has no solution.

x^2 + 4x + 4 + x^2 - 4x + 4 / (x - 2)(x + 2) = 0

$2x^2$ + 8 / (x - 2)(x + 2) = 0 => $2x^2$ + 8 = 0
x^2 + 4 = 0
$x_{1,2}$ = 0 $\pm$ $\sqrt{-4 * 4}$ / 2
$x_{1,2}$ = 0 $\pm$ $\sqrt{-16}$ / 2
Solution for the square root of -16 is not a real number, so this equation has no solution.

7. D

We need to distribute the factors to the terms inside the related parenthesis:

5($3x^2$ - 2) - x^2(2 - 3x) = $15x^2$ - 10 - ($2x^2$ - $3x^3$)

= $15x^2$ - 10 - $2x^2$ + $3x^3$

= $3x^3$ + $15x^2$ - $2x^2$ - 10 ... similar terms written together to ease summing/substituting.

$= 3x^3 + 13x^2 - 10$

8. B
We need to distribute the factors to the terms inside the related parenthesis:

$(x^3 + 2)(x^2 - x) - x^5 = x^5 - x^4 + (2x^2 - 2x) - x^5$

$= x^5 - x^4 + 2x^2 - 2x - x^5$

$= x^5 - x^5 - x^4 + 2x^2 - 2x$ ... similar terms written together to ease summing/substituting.

$= -x^4 + 2x^2 - 2x$

9. B
To simplify the expression, we need to find common factors. We see that both terms contain the term ab^2. So, we can take this term out of each term as a factor:
$ab^2 (9 + 8) = 17ab^2$

10. C
$x^2 - 7x - 30 = 0$ ... We try to separate the middle term $-7x$ to find common factors with x^2 and -30 separately:

$x^2 - 10x + 3x - 30 = 0$ ... Here, we see that x is a common factor for x^2 and $-10x$, and 3 is a common factor for $3x$ and -30:

$x(x - 10) + 3(x - 10) = 0$ ... Here, we have x times $x - 10$ and 3 times $x - 10$ summed up. This means that we have $x + 3$ times $x - 10$:

$(x + 3)(x - 10) = 0$ or $(x - 10)(x + 3) = 0$

11. A
We need to simplify the equation by distributing factors and then collecting x terms on one side, and the others on the other side:

$(a + 2)x - b = -2 + (a + b)x$

$ax + 2x - b = -2 + ax + bx$

$ax + 2x - ax - bx = -2 + b$ ... ax and -ax cancel each other:

$2x - bx = -2 + b$ ... we take -1 as a factor on the right side:

$(2 - b)x = -(2 - b)$

$x = -(2 - b)/(2 - b)$ ... Simplifying by $2 - b$:

$x = -1$

12. C
We are asked to find $A + B - C$. By paying attention to the sign distribution; we write the polynomials and operate:

$A + B - C = (-2x^4 + x^2 - 3x) + (x^4 - x^3 + 5) - (x^4 + 2x^3 + 4x + 5)$

$= -2x^4 + x^2 - 3x + x^4 - x^3 + 5 - x^4 - 2x^3 - 4x - 5$

$= -2x^4 + x^4 - x^4 - x^3 - 2x^3 + x^2 - 3x - 4x + 5 - 5$ ... similar terms written together to ease summing/substituting.

$= -2x^4 - 3x^3 + x^2 - 7x$

13. D
To simplify, we remove parenthesis:

$(4y^3 - 2y^2) + (7y^2 + 3y - y) = 4y^3 - 2y^2 + 7y^2 + 3y - y$ ... Then, we operate within similar terms:

$= 4y^3 + (-2 + 7)y^2 + (3 - 1)y = 4y^3 + 5y^2 + 2y$

14. C
To obtain a polynomial, we should remove the parenthesis by distributing the related factors to the terms inside the parenthesis:
$1 - x(1 - x(1 - x)) = 1 - x(1 - (x - x \bullet x)) = 1 - x(1 - x + x^2)$

$= 1 - (x - x \bullet x + x \bullet x^2) = 1 - x + x^2 - x^3$ ... Writing this result in descending order of powers:

$= -x^3 + x^2 - x + 1$

15. D
To simplify the expression, remove the parenthesis by distributing the related factors to the terms inside the parenthesis:

$7(2y + 8) + 1 - 4(y + 5) = (7 \bullet 2y + 7 \bullet 8) + 1 - (4 \bullet y + 4 \bullet 5)$

= 14y + 56 + 1 - 4y - 20

= 14y - 4y + 56 + 1 - 20 ... similar terms written together to ease summing/substituting.

= 10y + 37

16. D
We understand that each of the n employees earn s amount of salary weekly. This means that one employee earns s salary weekly. So; Richard has ns amount of money to employ n employees for a week.

We are asked to find the number of days n employees can be employed with x amount of money. We can do simple direct proportion:

If Richard can employ n employees for 7 days with ns amount of money,

Richard can employ n employees for y days with x amount of money ... y is the number of days we need to find.

We can do cross multiplication:

y = (x•7)/(ns)

y = 7x/ns

17. A
x^2 - 3x - 4 ... We try to separate the middle term -3x to find common factors with x^2 and -4 separately:

x^2 + x - 4x - 4 ... Here, we see that x is a common factor for x^2 and x, and -4 is a common factor for -4x and -4:

= x(x + 1) - 4(x + 1) ... Here, we have x times x + 1 and -4 times x + 1 summed up. This means that we have x - 4 times x + 1:

= (x - 4)(x + 1) or (x + 1)(x - 4)

18. D
We need to simplify and have x alone and on one side in order to solve the inequality:

$(2x + 1)/(2x - 1) < 1$

$(2x + 1)/(2x - 1) - 1 < 0$ ... We need to write the left side at the common denominator $2x - 1$:

$(2x + 1)/(2x - 1) - (2x - 1)/(2x - 1) < 0$

$(2x + 1 - 2x + 1)/(2x - 1) < 0$ ... $2x$ and $-2x$ terms cancel each other in the numerator:

$2/(2x - 1) < 0$

2 is a positive number; so,

$2x - 1 < 0$

$2x < 1$

$x < 1/2$ ... This means that x should be smaller than $1/2$ and not equal to $1/2$. This is shown as $(-\infty, 1/2)$.

19. D

To solve the equation, we need the equation in the form $ax^2 + bx + c = 0$.

$(a^2 - b^2)x^2 + 2ax + 1 = 0$ is already in this form.

The quadratic formula to find the roots of a quadratic equation is:

$x_{1,2} = (-b \pm \sqrt{\Delta}) / 2a$ where $\Delta = b^2 - 4ac$ and is called the discriminant of the quadratic equation.

In our question, the equation is $(a^2 - b^2)x^2 + 2ax + 1 = 0$.

By remembering the form $ax^2 + bx + c = 0$: $a = a^2 - b^2$, $b = 2a$, $c = 1$

So, we can find the discriminant first, and then the roots of the equation:

$\Delta = b^2 - 4ac = (2a)^2 - 4(a^2 - b^2)\cdot 1 = 4a^2 - 4a^2 + 4b^2 = 4b^2$

$x_{1,2} = (-b \pm \sqrt{\Delta}) / 2a = (-2a \pm \sqrt{4b^2}) / (2(a^2 - b^2)) = (-2a \pm 2b) / (2(a^2 - b^2))$

$= 2(-a \pm b) / (2(a^2 - b^2))$ ... We can simplify by 2:

$= (-a \pm b) / (a^2 - b^2)$

This means that the roots are,

$x_1 = (-a - b) / (a^2 - b^2)$ ... $a^2 - b^2$ is two square differences:

$x_1 = -(a + b) / ((a - b)(a + b))$ ... $(a + b)$ terms cancel each other:

$x_1 = -1/(a - b)$

$x_2 = (-a + b) / (a^2 - b^2)$ ... $a^2 - b^2$ is two square differences:

$x_2 = -(a - b) / ((a - b)(a + b))$ ... $(a - b)$ terms cancel each other:

$x_2 = -1/(a + b)$

20. A
To simplify, we need to remove the parenthesis and see if any terms cancel:

$(a + b)(x + y) + (a - b)(x - y) - (ax + by) = ax + ay + bx + by + ax - ay - bx + by - ax - by$

By writing similar terms together:

$= ax + ax - ax + bx - bx + ay - ay + by + by - by$ ... + terms cancel - terms:

$= ax + by$

21. C
We are asked to add polynomials A + B. By paying attention to the sign distribution; we write the polynomials and operate:

$A + B = (4x^5 - 2x^2 + 3x - 2) + (-3x^4 - 5x^2 - 4x + 5)$

$= 4x^5 - 2x^2 + 3x - 2 - 3x^4 - 5x^2 - 4x + 5$ ... Writing similar terms together:

$= 4x^5 - 3x^4 - 2x^2 - 5x^2 + 3x - 4x - 2 + 5$ ... Operating within similar terms:

$= 4x^5 - 3x^4 - 7x^2 - x + 3$

22. B
Total Volume = Volume of large cylinder - Volume of small cylinder

Volume of a cylinder = area of base • height = $\pi r^2 \cdot h$

Total Volume = $(\pi \cdot 12^2 \cdot 10) - (\pi \cdot 6^2 \cdot 5) = 1440\pi - 180\pi$

$= 1260\pi$ in^3

23. A
Slope (m) = $\dfrac{\text{change in y}}{\text{change in x}}$

If we know the coordinates of two points on a line, we can find the slope (m) with the below formula:

m = $(y_2 - y_1)/(x_2 - x_1)$ where (x_1, y_1) represent the coordinates of one point and (x_2, y_2) the other.

In this question:

$(-9, 6) : x_1 = -9, y_1 = 6$

$(18, -18) : x_2 = 18, y_2 = -18$

Inserting these values into the formula:

m = $(-18 - 6)/(18 - (-9)) = (-24)/(27)$ ... Simplifying by 3:

m = $-8/9$

24. A
If we know the coordinates of two points on a line, we can find the slope (m) with the below formula:
m = $(y_2 - y_1)/(x_2 - x_1)$ where (x_1, y_1) represent the coordinates of one point and (x_2, y_2) the other.

In this question:

$(-4, y_1) : x_1 = -4, y_1 =$ we will find

$(-8, 7) : x_2 = -8, y_2 = 7$

m = $-7/4$

Inserting these values into the formula:

$-7/4 = (7 - y_1)/(-8 - (-4))$

$-7/4 = (7 - y_1)/(-8 + 4)$

$7/(-4) = (7 - y_1)/(-4)$ ... Simplifying the denominators of both sides by -4:

$7 = 7 - y_1$

$0 = -y_1$

$y_1 = 0$

25. D

The area of a rectangle is found by multiplying the width to the length. If we call these sides with "a" and "b"; the area is = a•b.

We are given that a•b = 20 cm² ... Equation I

One side is increased by 1 and the other by 2 cm. So new side lengths are "a + 1" and "b + 2".

The new area is (a + 1)(b + 2) = 35 cm² ... Equation II

Using equations I and II, we can find a and b:

$ab = 20$

(a + 1)(b + 2) = 35 ... We need to distribute the terms in parenthesis:

$ab + 2a + b + 2 = 35$

We can insert ab = 20 to the above equation:

$20 + 2a + b + 2 = 35$

$2a + b = 35 - 2 - 20$

2a + b = 13 ... This is one equation with two unknowns. We need to use another information to have two equations with two unknowns which leads us to the solution. We know that ab = 20. So, we can use a = 20/b:

2(20/b) + b = 13

40/b + b = 13 ... We equate all denominators to "b" and eliminate it:

40 + b^2 = 13b

b^2 - 13b + 40 = 0 ... We can use the roots by factoring. We try to separate the middle term -13b to find common factors with b^2 and 40 separately:

b^2 - 8b - 5b + 40 = 0 ⋯ Here, we see that b is a common factor for b^2 and -8b, and -5 is a common factor for -5b and 40:

b(b - 8) - 5(b - 8) = 0 Here, we have b times b - 8 and -5 times b - 8 summed up. This means that we have b - 5 times b - 8:

(b - 5)(b - 8) = 0

This is true when either or both of the expressions in the parenthesis are equal to zero:

b - 5 = 0 ... b = 5

b - 8 = 0 ... b = 8

So we have two values for b which means we have two values for a as well. In order to find a, we can use any equation we have. Let us use a = 20/b.

If b = 5, a = 20/b -> a = 4

If b = 8, a = 20/b -> a = 2.5

So, (a, b) pairs for the sides of the original rectangle are: (4, 5) and (2.5, 8). These are found in (b) and (c) answer choices.

26. D
The distance between two points is found by = $[(x_2 - x_1)^2 + (y_2 - y_1)^2]^{1/2}$

In this question:

(18, 12) : x_1 = 18, y_1 = 12

(9, -6) : x_2 = 9, y_2 = -6

Distance= $[(9 - 18)^2 + (-6 - 12)^2]^{1/2}$

= $[(-9)^2 + (-18)^2]^{1/2}$

= $(9^2 + 2^2 \cdot 9^2)^{1/2}$

= $(9^2(1 + 5))^{1/2}$ ... We can take 9 out of the square root:

= $9 \cdot 6^{1/2}$

= $9\sqrt{6}$

= $9 \cdot 2.45$

= 22.04

The distance is approximately 22 units.

27. D
$1/(4x - 2)$ = 5/6 ... We can do cross multiplication:
$5(4x - 2)$ = 1•6 ... Now, we distribute 5 to the parenthesis:

20x - 10 = 6 ... We need x term alone on one side:

20x = 6 + 10

20x = 16 ... Dividing both sides by 20:

x = 16/20 ... Simplifying by 2 and having 10 in the denominator provides us finding the decimal equivalent of x:

x = 8/10 = 0.8

28. A
The formula of the volume of cylinder is the base area multiplied by the height. As the formula:

Volume of a cylinder = $\pi r^2 h$. Where π is 3.142, r is radius of the cross sectional area, and h is the height.

We know that the diameter is 5 meters, so the radius is 5/2

= 2.5 meters.

The volume is: $V = 3.142 \cdot 2.5^2 \cdot 12 = 235.65$ m^3.

29. C

The large cube is made up of 8 smaller cubes with 5 cm sides. The volume of a cube is found by the third power of the length of one side.
Volume of the large cube = Volume of the small cube•8

$= (5^3) \cdot 8 = 125 \cdot 8$

$= 1000$ cm^3

There is another solution for this question. Find the side length of the large cube. There are two cubes rows with 5 cm length for each. So, one side of the large cube is 10 cm.

The volume of this large cube is equal to $10^3 = 1000$ cm^3

30. A

First write the two equations one under the other. Our aim is to multiply equations with appropriate factors to eliminate one unknown and find the other, and then find the eliminated one using the found value.

$-\sqrt{5} / x\sqrt{5} - y = \sqrt{5}$ ... If we multiply this equation by $\sqrt{5}$, y terms will cancel each other:

$\underline{x - y\sqrt{5} = 5}$

$-x\sqrt{5}\sqrt{5} + y\sqrt{5} = -\sqrt{5}\sqrt{5}$ ... using $\sqrt{5}\sqrt{5} = 5$:

$\underline{x - y\sqrt{5} = 5}$

$-5x + y\sqrt{5} = -5$

$\underline{x - y\sqrt{5} = 5}$ ... Summing side-by-side:

$-5x + y\sqrt{5} + x - y\sqrt{5} = -5 + 5$ ... $+ y\sqrt{5}$ and $- y\sqrt{5}$, -5 and $+ 5$ cancel each other:

$-4x = 0$

$x = 0$

Now, using either of the equations gives us the value of y. Let us choose equation 1:

$x\sqrt{5} - y = \sqrt{5}$

$0\sqrt{5} - y = \sqrt{5}$

$-y = \sqrt{5}$

$y = -\sqrt{5}$

The solution to the system is $(0, -\sqrt{5})$

Writing

1. D
"Who" is correct because the question uses an active construction. "To whom was first place given?" is passive construction.

2. D
"Which" is correct, because the files are objects and not people.

3. C
The simple present tense, "rises," is correct.

4. A
"Lie" does not require a direct object, while "lay" does. The old woman might lie on the couch, which has no direct object, or she might lay the book down, which has the direct object, "the book."

5. D
The simple present tense, "falls," is correct because it is repeated action.

6. A
The present progressive, "building models," is correct in this sentence; it is required to match the other present progressive verbs.

7. C
Past Perfect tense describes a completed action in the past, before another action in the past.

8. D
The preposition "to" is the correct preposition to use with "bring."

9. D
"Laid" is the past tense.

10. A
This is a past unreal conditional sentence. It requires an 'if' clause and a result clause, and either clause can appear first. The 'if' clause uses the past perfect, while the result clause uses the past participle.

11. C
Bring vs. Take. Usage depends on your location. Something coming your way is brought to you. Something going away is taken from you.

12. A
The sentence is correct. Went vs. Gone. Went is the simple past tense. Gone is used in the past perfect.

13. B
Fewer vs. Less. 'Fewer' is used with countables and 'less' is used with uncountables.

14. B
His father is a poet and a novelist. It is necessary to use 'a' twice in this sentence for the two distinct things.

15. C
The semicolon links independent clauses. An independent clause can form a complete sentence by itself.

16. A
The semicolon links independent clauses with a conjunction (However).

17. B
The sentence is correct. The semicolon links independent clauses. An independent clause can form a complete sentence by itself.

18. A
The third conditional is used for talking about an unreal situation (that did not happen) in the past. For example, "If I had studied harder, [if clause] I would have passed the exam [main clause]. Which is the same as, "I failed the exam, because I didn't study hard enough."

19. B
Here the word "sale" is used as a "word" and not as a word in the sentence, so quotation marks are used.

20. C
Titles of short stories are enclosed in quotation marks, and commas always go inside quotation marks.

21. A
Quoted speech is not capitalized.

22. B
The verb raise ('to increase', 'to lift up.') can appear in three forms, raise, raised and raised.

23. C
The two verbs "shall" and "will" should not be used in the same sentence when referring to the same future.

24. B
When two subjects are linked with "with" or "as well," use the verb form that matches the first subject.

25. A
Use a plural verb for nouns like measles, tongs, trousers, riches, scissors etc.

26. C
A verb can fit any of the two subjects in a compound sentence since the verb form agrees with that subject.

27. C
Always use the singular verb form for nouns like politics, wages, mathematics, innings, news, advice, summons, furniture, information, poetry, machinery, vacation, scenery etc.

28. C
Always use the singular verb form for nouns like politics, wages, mathematics, innings, news, advice, summons, furniture, information, poetry, machinery, vacation, scenery etc.

29. A
Use a singular verb with a plural noun that refers to a specific amount or quantity that is considered as a whole (dozen, hundred score etc).

30. C
Use a singular verb with either, each, neither, everyone and many.

Conclusion

CONGRATULATIONS! You have made it this far because you have applied yourself diligently to practicing for the exam and no doubt improved your potential score considerably! Getting into a good school is a huge step in a journey that might be challenging at times but will be many times more rewarding and fulfilling. That is why being prepared is so important.

Good Luck!

FREE Ebook Version

Download a FREE Ebook version of the publication!

Suitable for tablets, iPad, iPhone, or any smart phone.

Go to
http://www.tinyurl.com/l8db4mb

Register for Free Updates and More Practice Test Questions

Register your purchase at www.test-preparation.ca/register.html for fast and convenient access to updates, errata, free test tips and more practice test questions.

PERT Test Strategy!

Learn to increase your score using time-tested secrets for answering multiple choice questions!

This practice book has everything you need to know about answering multiple choice questions on a standardized test!

You will learn 12 strategies for answering multiple choice questions and then practice each strategy with over 45 reading comprehension multiple choice questions, with extensive commentary from exam experts!

Maybe you have read this kind of thing before, and maybe feel you don't need it, and you are not sure if you are going to buy this Book.

Remember though, it only a few percentage points divide the PASS from the FAIL students.

Even if our multiple choice strategies increase your score by a few percentage points, isn't that worth it?

Go to

https://www.createspace.com/4610546

Enter Code LYFZGQB5 for 25% off!

Get Organized, Study Less and Get Higher Marks!

Here is what you will learn:

- How to Organize your Study Space

- Four different strategies for taking notes

- Reading strategies for textbooks, essays, novels and literature

- How to Concentrate - What is concentration and how do you do it!

- Using Flash Cards - Complete guide to using flash cards including the Leitner method.

and LOT more... Including time management, sleep, nutrition, motivation, brain food, procrastination, study schedules and more!

Go to

https://www.createspace.com/4060298

Enter Code LYFZGQB5 for 25% off!

Endnotes

Reading Comprehension passages where noted below are used under the Creative Commons Attribution-ShareAlike 3.0 License

http://en.wikipedia.org/wiki/Wikipedia:Text_of_Creative_Commons_Attribution-ShareAlike_3.0_Unported_License

[1] Infectious disease. In *Wikipedia*. Retrieved November 12, 2010 from http://en.wikipedia.org/wiki/Infectious_disease.
[2] Thunderstorm. In *Wikipedia*. Retrieved November 12, 2010 from en.wikipedia.org/wiki/Thunderstorm.
[3] Meteorology. In *Wikipedia*. Retrieved November 12, 2010 from en.wikipedia.org/wiki/Outline_of_meteorology.
[4] Cloud. In *Wikipedia*. Retrieved November 12, 2010 from http://en.wikipedia.org/wiki/Clouds.
[5] Mary Shelley, Frankenstein, In Gutenberg. Retrieved October 13, 2014 http://www.gutenberg.org/files/84/84-h/84-h.htm
[6] Tree. In *Wikipedia*. Retrieved November 12, 2010 from http://en.wikipedia.org/wiki/Tree.
[7] Respiratory System. In *Wikipedia*. Retrieved November 12, 2010 from en.wikipedia.org/wiki/Respiratory_system.
[8] Lightning. In *Wikipedia*. Retrieved November 12, 2010 from http://en.wikipedia.org/wiki/Lightning.
[9] Mythology. In *Wikipedia*. Retrieved November 12, 2010 from en.wikipedia.org/wiki/Mythology.
[10] U.S. Navy Seal. In *Wikipedia*. Retrieved November 12, 2010 from en.wikipedia.org/wiki/United_States_Navy_SEALs.

CPSIA information can be obtained
at www.ICGtesting.com
Printed in the USA
FFOW04n1405050218
44939190-45179FF